To Sarah & [...] with love and [...] affection! Enjoy, Linda ♡

THE POWER OF COACHING

Manifesting Transformation in the World

BARBARA WAINWRIGHT

STOKE Publishing

STOKE Publishing

ISBN: 978-1-988675-27-5

Editor: Joanna Bell

This book is dedicated to Tracy Brown, Linda Gallicchio, Jennifer Sparks, and naturally all the authors, without whom this book would not exist.

Contents

Foreword

BY PRIN KAMP

I have known Barbara for eleven years, and I am grateful that she asked me to write the foreword for this book. I consider it an honor and a privilege. Barbara's goal is to awaken as many people as possible to the glory of God that is within them. Her philosophy is, through life coaching, that the more people who awaken to their divine purpose, the closer we will get to the tipping point where world peace is inevitable.

I was drawn into each story as the authors shared their personal experiences with coaching and how each of them had found their own unique way to becoming a professional coach. Each author brings their insights, personality, experiences, joys, triumphs, and struggles. I marvelled at how open and forthright the authors were in their willingness to bare their souls to help others to get started on their own path to self-discovery and self-love.

Each story is an in-depth look at the vast diversity of coaching including Cross-Cultural Business coaching, Anxiety and Stress Management coaching, Leadership coaching, Spiritual coaching,

Relationship coaching, Weight-Loss coaching, Life Purpose coaching and a whole host of other genres designed to encourage their clients to begin their own personal journeys. It was uplifting to read their stories.

In the ten minutes it takes to read each of these stories, you will learn more about yourself and which coaching genre will best serve you. This book is thought-provoking as it shares the many different aspects of coaching. Even though I have been coaching for years, many of these concepts were fresh and new to me.

If you are contemplating hiring a coach for your own personal growth, this book is a great resource to learn about some of the options in coaching available to you.

Again, my thanks goes to Barbara for putting out this work into the Universe and for making it possible for each of us to continue on our own paths towards love and peace.

Preface

This book idea is the result of a collaboration between myself, Tracy Brown, Linda Gallicchio, and Jennifer Sparks, who are all Certified Professional Coaches through Wainwright Global, Institute of Professional Coaching. I had wanted to create a book about coaching for decades. I just didn't know how. I also knew that it would require a lot of leg-work to get a book published.

As God would have it, Tracy came to me and asked how she could be of service. I received an email from Jennifer letting me know she had started a publishing company. And when it came time to review the chapters Linda found a new passion and immersed herself in reading each and every one of them.

Tracy and I had many discussions about different projects we could work on together. She threw out the idea for a book compilation of coaching stories and I said "Yes, I've been wanting to do that for years!" Coincidentally, shortly after our discussion, I received an email from Jennifer. She had just finished publishing a book for someone else and was now available to work on a new project. She was now available to do all the things required to get a book published on Amazon. Then as the chapters began to arrive from each of the authors, Linda volunteered to read each one. Soon after she had read the first few, she realized that she had uncovered a new passion for reading, editing, and providing feedback to each author.

The creation of this book has been full of grace and ease and I am forever grateful to these soulful women who made it possible.

With over ten years of training coaches how to coach, I have heard so many stories about how people's lives have been dramatically changed by the process of coaching. In my own life, coaching has been such a powerful catalyst for positive change that I want to spread the good news about the power of coaching to the world. What better way to share about coaching success stories than from the coaches themselves.

I trust you will enjoy reading each of these stories and that you will learn about the different coaching niches and how you can potentially benefit from hiring your own coach.

ONE

Don't Let Life Happen. Make Life Happen.

STOP DRIFTING AND START PAYING ATTENTION

By Kim Fowler

If you ignore something good in your life, you will lose it! If you want something better in your life, you have to work for it. You can't put anything in your life on autopilot.

I CAN'T REALLY PINPOINT the exact event that changed my life; it was more like a series of events. I was born to two "drifters." My parents weren't drifters in the traditional sense. They were drifters in life. Neither of them had the life they wanted because they ignored the opportunities life presented to them. I don't think they knew what they wanted in life. They had no plan, no vision, no clarity.

My dad married three times. His last wife died of a crack overdose. His career bored him. He did what he thought he was supposed to do and paid little attention to anything. He went through the motions. I don't think he was ever truly happy.

My mother had a few jobs during her life. None of them lasted more than six months. She attended three different colleges, but never graduated. She lived off the memories of her glory days when she was a straight "A" high school student and prom queen.

When I was three years old, my parents divorced. I lived with my mom, and she soon married a wonderful man who was a Navy captain. We moved across the country, leaving behind my father, grandparents, and friends. Over the next ten years, we moved every eighteen months, leaving behind old friends and making new ones. By the time I graduated high school, I had attended twelve different schools, and I experienced lots of change—new cities, countries, schools, and people. I learned to adapt to change quickly and realized that opportunity was everywhere.

My mother and stepfather divorced when I was a junior in high school. I was crushed. My mother committed suicide the following year. She blamed me in the note she left behind.

I wish I could say I handled it well. I didn't. It was a bumpy ride that year following my mother's death. I made some incredibly poor decisions during that time. I was stuck and could not move forward. I was in a downward spiral, headed nowhere. I was drifting, hanging out with a "bad" crowd, working in a dead-end job, skipping more college classes than I attended. To make matters worse, I discovered that my boyfriend was married, and he was dealing drugs.

The downward spiral continued when I was arrested for a DUI and spent a night in jail. It was the wake-up call I needed.

I had to change my behavior and my life. I was drifting, just as my parents had, ignoring everything good in my life, and paying attention to all the wrong things. I had no plan, and I was floundering.

I blamed my mother for my situation. I felt guilty, and that was her fault. I had to work for a living instead of becoming a full-time college student. Her fault. I blamed her because I had to skip classes because of work. I blamed her because I drank too much and got behind the wheel of a car. I played the blame game instead of taking responsibility for my own actions. I gave myself zero power over my own life.

Drawing on the positive experiences from my childhood, I started making a plan. To get serious about going to school, I knew I had to get away from my friends and the beach. So I packed up my car and drove 180 miles to Tallahassee, Florida. I found an apartment and a roommate. I enrolled at a community college, intending to later transfer to Florida State University. I worked two part-time jobs.

Things were improving, and I began taking my life for granted. I was running on autopilot. My vision became murky.

I started dating someone. We dated for two years, and then he gave me an ultimatum. (You can guess where this is going.) We married as soon as I graduated from school. I knew it was the wrong decision. Our marriage lasted eighteen stormy months.

After the divorce, I recognized that I had stopped appreciating and paying attention to what I had in my life. I had to get back to my vision.

Once I got clear about what I wanted, opportunities began to present themselves. Successes came quickly. I started working as an advertising director for a restaurant chain. I went on to work as a regional marketing director for a large corporation and later at a trade association. I started my own business and sold it within two years.

I stopped drifting and started paying attention to what was going on around me. I started appreciating the people in my life who cared about me. I knew what I was capable of achieving and stopped wasting time. I went back to school at the age of forty to get my MBA. I stopped caring what others thought or said about me, and I refused to let negativity cloud my thoughts.

I became a life coach to help people create the lives they want by overcoming their own setbacks and defining their vision. I help clients understand their impact and their potential, so that they stop selling themselves short. They gain clarity and confidence, and become more successful than they ever imagined. They take exotic vacations, start successful businesses, and leave toxic relationships, all because they stop drifting through their daily routines and start paying attention to what is important in their lives. They take advantage of more opportunities because they are living with purpose and intention.

Matt worked as a restaurant bartender. He was bored and disillusioned with his job. He came to me because he was drifting and didn't know what he wanted. When we dug into what was going on in his life, it was clear that he had work to do on issues beyond his dissatisfaction in his job. He was in a disastrous relationship and a living situation that he couldn't afford to leave. His family was five hours away and he missed them.

Matt ignored the real issues so he didn't have to deal with them. He was going through the motions. He was drifting. And he was ignoring the good things in his life. He had friends who cared about him. He had a family who loved him and wanted him to come home. He was an amazing cook and had a passion for it. Matt didn't realize the great things he had because he wasn't paying attention. He knew he wanted change, but didn't know what or how to change, because he wasn't living with purpose.

Within months of us working together, Matt landed a job in a five-star restaurant, working under the head chef. A few months later, a friend loaned him money to buy a food truck. He moved home to his friends and family and started a successful food truck business. All this happened within fifteen months because he stopped drifting, started paying attention to the right things, and made his life happen!

You will lose the good in your life if you ignore it. If you want something better in your life, you have to work for it. You can't live your life on autopilot.

Here are three lessons I learned the hard way:

- **Pay Attention.** You are responsible for your life. Only you can create the results that you want. Whether it's a great relationship or good health, don't put anything in your life on autopilot. Stop mindlessly going through your routine. Notice the opportunities and resources that will help you get what you truly want.

- **If You Ignore It, You Will Lose It!** Ignore your friends and family, you could find yourself alone and miserable. Ignore your health, and you could end up in the hospital. Ignore your finances, and you may end up broke. Appreciate what you have now. Be grateful for what you have today. Don't take anything for granted. Get clear about what you want and stop ignoring what is important in your life.

- **Make Life Happen.** Don't drift through life. Don't let drifting get the better of you. Drifting leads to confusion. There is no clear destination. And without a clear destination, we fail to see the opportunities that are all around us. Don't regret the action not taken. Make real changes in your life. Know where you are going. Live with purpose and intention.

What is drifting in your life? Once you know the answer, do one thing today that will move you closer to your destination.

Remember, life is a journey.

Meet Kim Fowler

Kim Fowler is the founder of Fowler Life Coaching, LLC. Her passion is helping people take charge of their lives to realize their full potential. She also works with businesses to motivate teams and reinforce their visions for strategic planning.

Kim is a certified professional life coach, speaker and author who contributes monthly to *South Carolina Woman* magazine and *Transitions* magazine. She has over fifteen years of life coaching experience and started her own practice in 2008. She has her MBA from George Mason University, and became interested in the life coaching field because of her own chaotic childhood. Kim is passionate about helping people strengthen their confidence so they can leap forward and shine. She has helped individuals triumph in many difficult situations.

Currently, Kim serves as president of Women in Networking of South Carolina (WIN), and is a member of the International Association of Coaching (IAC). She also holds several volunteer positions in the community. She lives in Surfside Beach, SC with her husband and five rescue cats. For more information about Kim or to download her free eBook *Design the Life You Were Meant to Have*, go to fowlercoaching.com.

TWO

Gaining Insights into a Purpose-Filled Life

IN HELPING ANOTHER, I FOUND MY PURPOSE

By Dr. Dawn A. Peters-Bascombe

God has led me towards a purpose-filled life. It is true that one thing leads to another. In living a life of service to God, he transformed my life into serving others.

THE REASON for living stood out clearly in my mind five years ago on that day when a young female friend came to my home office. As she entered the office and sat down, she seemed rather upset and it was not long after that she began to cry inconsolably. Anna-Louise was a teenage mother of a one-year-old daughter and although she resided with the baby's father, he was abusive and was not a reliable source of support. At that time, she was attending a community college program and was in the first year of the early years program. Anna-Louise stated that it was her dream to complete this program and get a better paying job to support her young daughter. She verbalized that being a teenage mother and a student at the same time was overwhelming without the appropriate support in place. She stated that she was falling behind with her course work and was worried that she was not going to make the grade to complete the year.

As I listened to her concern, I tried my best to console her but nothing seemed to work. I empathized with her and her situation, especially when she stated that she felt as though she was a failure. I believed that if I opened up about the struggles that I experienced when raising my four young children as a divorced parent, that I might help her. I dug deep into my past and talked about the strategies that I used in managing my life, school, work, and the children. During my talking, I must have said something that reached her because at that moment she stopped crying, lifted her head, and looked at me in the face. This was a breakthrough opportunity. I handed her a Kleenex; she wiped her face. At that time I said, "Yes, you are looking at a single mother who was sitting in the same seat many years ago, but the only difference was that I had four children." I was not trying to make light of her situation, but I wanted her to know that life as a single parent was not easy and that I empathized with her. I informed her that there were people in my life at that time that held my hand and eased my heavy load. However, above all, spiritually, I was never alone on that journey because God was there and led me all the way.

Insight into Life's Purpose

Anna-Louise began to open up more about her situation. Seeing that we shared similar experiences, it was easy for me to relate to her. It was crucial for me to listen and to provide support at that difficult time. She continued to share her concerns with me for another forty-five minutes on that day. As I was listening to her concern, I observed how relaxed she had become while communicating with me. I felt comfortable with listening and at the same time demonstrating a compassionate and a caring attitude towards her. I felt very comfortable in the supporting role. Over the next year after that initial meeting, Anna-Louise made weekly telephone calls to me to speak about her progress and to bounce ideas off me. She successfully completed the program and made another visit to my home office to thank me for my support in helping her to reach her goal. She said, "Now I can find a job and begin to live my dream. Thank you for being a great listener." This was a big moment for me; I had done something in my life that made a big difference in someone else's life. At that very moment there was a revelation and true meaning of why I was placed on this earth. I received an insight into my purpose in life. Until that day, I truly did not know what my life's purpose was.

The Importance of Knowing One's Life Purpose

Heisel and Flett (2004) stated that when one lacks a sense of purpose in life this is associated with mental ill-being. Bonebright, Clay, and Ankenmann's (2000) study found that having a purpose in life is very important to a person's well-being and to his or her survival. According to Park et al. (as cited in Rainey, 2014) many psychologists believed that for most of us, our purpose is not naturally known—most of us were born without knowing what our purpose in life is. They also believe that we must find, create, or learn about our purpose. However, Rainey (2014) found that those people at older ages were more likely to have found their purpose in life than those at younger ages. This is definitely my case.

Prior to the experience with Anna-Louise, although I lacked the knowledge of what my purpose in life was, God knew it all along. This assurance is written in Jeremiah 1:5 which states, "I knew you before I formed you in your mother's womb. Before you were born, I set you apart and appointed you as my prophet to the nations." God has brought me across the world in preparation for my life's purpose. My journey as a registered nurse began in my early twenties when I emigrated from the small island of St. Vincent and the Grenadines to pursue my nursing career. I studied in the United Kingdom, Canada, and the United States. Today, I hold a Bachelor of Science in Nursing, a Master of Science in Nursing, and a Doctor of Education/Health Policy. Despite my many successes, there were years of rocky road with my marriage breakdown and being a single parent of four children. I believe that even then, through my difficult times in life, God was preparing me for the work ahead.

Along the journey, I met many people and gained many experiences. Today I feel that I am prepared to answer any questions, to deal with many situations that I encounter, and I am equipped with the tools to get the work done. Since my experience with Anna-Louise, I often look for opportunity to lend a helping hand; any opportunity that will empower others, I am there. I am in that place in my life where I get the opportunity to help students, colleagues, friends, family, and members of my community. I use this as my chance to give back. As cited in the National College for Teaching and Leadership (2013), a Swahili proverb stated that, "The greatest gift we can give to others is not just to share our riches with them, but to reveal their riches to themselves."

Today, when I encounter a person who is confused as to which path in life he or she should choose, I have a burning desire to listen, to empower, and to build that individual. Looking back to that moment of revelation with the experience with Anna-Louise, it all makes sense now as to how God has groomed me for the role of a coach, a nurse, and an educator. I often smile when something that is so familiar to one of my life experiences shows its head because I am always ready. I am certain that my goal in life correlates with my values and beliefs and this is definitely my reason for living.

Conclusion

The experience with Anna-Louise has taught me to explore the meaning of my life purpose. Many of our young people are turning to drugs and alcohol and suicide to find peace. They are wandering aimlessly throughout life without knowing the reason behind their true existence. The only difference with me was that I consciously chose to serve God and he paved the way for the rest of my life. Coaching is important in helping individuals to find their purpose in life, to decrease unnecessary sufferings. As a coach, my goal is to empower others to solve their life problem and to be the best that they can be. Victor Frankl (as cited in Talpursky, 2014) stated that the idea that the source of life meaning and purpose lies within ourselves as individuals, and Nelson Mandela (as cited in Gihring, 2013) stated that "There is no passion to be found in playing small—in settling for a life that is less than the one you are capable of living."

One very important thing that is missing in our lives today is the need for the presence of God and the help of a coach. The big questions are: "Do you believe in the power of coaching? Or do you believe that a coach can help you to gain an insight into your purpose in life?"

References

Bonebright, C. A., Clay, D. L., & Ankenmann, R. D. (2000). The relationship of workaholism with work–life conflict, life satisfaction, and purpose in life. *Journal of Counseling Psychology, 47*(4), 469-477.

Gihring, T. (2013). *Art and activism: Nelson Mandela's fight for free expression.* Minneapolis Institute of Art. Retrieved from https://new.artsmia.org/stories/nelson-mandela-and-the-arts-fighting-together-for-freedom/

Heisel, M. J., & Flett, G. L. (2004). Purpose in life, satisfaction with life, and suicide ideation in a clinical sample. *Journal of Psychopathology and Behavioral Assessment, 26*(2), 127-135.

National College for Teaching and Leadership. (2013). *Think piece: Empowering others: Coaching and mentoring.* Retrieved from https://www.nationalcollege.org.uk/cm-mc-mccor-tp.pdf

Talpursky, G. (2014). *Searching for meaning and purpose in life? Religion is optional.* Retrieved from http://intentionalinsights.org/searching-for-meaning-and-purpose-in-life-religion-is-optional/

Meet Dr. Dawn Peters-Bascombe

Professional Background

Dr. Peters-Bascombe, a Certified Professional Coach, is a nurse educator with Ryerson University and George Brown College in Ontario, Canada. She is a high-performing healthcare professional with many years of experience in the fields of Nursing, Management, and Education.

Education and Experience

Dr. Peters-Bascombe holds a Bachelor of Science in Nursing from Ryerson University, Ontario, Canada; a Master of Science in Nursing, and a Doctor of Education and Health Policy from D'Youville College, New York, U.S.A. Dr. Peters-Bascombe has worked with several prestigious healthcare institutions in Canada and the

United States and has coached clients, students, and members of various communities.

Personal Details

Dr. Peters-Bascombe, born in St. Vincent and the Grenadines, currently resides in Ontario, Canada with her children. She gained insight into a purpose-filled life five years ago, and since that time she vowed to spend her life empowering others to solve life problems and to become the best that they can be. In this book, *The Power of Coaching*, Dr. Peters-Bascombe stated that she has made one conscious decision in her life and that is to serve God and in turn serve others. Dr. Peters-Bascombe can be reached at dawn-peters07@yahoo.com.

THREE

Restoration After a Perfect Storm

THE POWER OF A LEADER-COACH TO RESTORE A
TEAM'S PERFORMANCE AND REPUTATION

By Linda Callecod

*We knew that if we wanted our stakeholders and clients to see us
differently, we first had to see ourselves differently—both individually
and collectively.*

EVERYONE LOVES A GREAT RAGS-TO-RICHES STORY. All the more,
we're encouraged when we see the before and after photos of the
person who lost 250 pounds, started their own business, then went
from rags to riches while still in their thirties. It gives us a sense of
empowerment and hope for our own situation to improve. We
believe that if *they* could do it, *we* can too!

What these great stories have in common is what takes place
between the "before" and the "after": it's hard work—no substi-
tutes, no gimmicks, and no magic pills. If we took a closer look,
we'd also see that the ones who successfully sustained their victory
did not make their journey alone—they had coaches!

To take a team from a place of unhappy, unproductive, and dysfunctional defeatism to a happy place of creativity, motivation, and extraordinary achievement would be to embark on a journey of hard work and perseverance. This team would need a leader-coach: one who could proficiently use tools of curious inquiry, esteem building, strategic thinking, consensus building, teaming, counseling, incentivizing, reshaping mindsets, and andragogic theory. Whew!

Let me make it clear: in this dual role, the leader-coach would need a *lot* of skill. As leader, he/she would set the pace, define the goal, set metrics, create efficacy, and lead the way while clearing the path for the team to follow. He/she would also ensure that operational systems were in place and working efficiently to support the team's success. As coach, he/she would help to develop and strengthen the skills and talents of team members—individually and collectively—and provide tools and opportunities to practice until achieving mastery-level competency. He/she would also provide guidance that enhanced night-vision, enabling the team to see their way through dark patches of difficulty and uncertainty.

This work is not for the faint of heart, but for the empathic brave. The leader-coach must, therefore, come to the table fully armed with trustworthiness, emotional intelligence, a vision worth the buy-in, competency, and a good plan. All doable!

Here's an example of recovery after a perfect storm—a challenge I couldn't resist:

The Setting

The training department of a large conglomerate imploded due to poor decision-making, a change in senior management, disorganization, favoritism, and unethical behavior by a vice president and several team members. Many were fired, the department disgraced, and all that remained after the storm was a training manager and a part-time administrative assistant. The proverbial "smoke" was still clearing even as my leadership appointment as director was being negotiated.

Re-building the Team

My first task, after inheriting this team, was to create a safe environment of trust. I took my two remaining direct-reports to lunch to get acquainted, and to understand what they felt and thought about what happened. I asked for their help and partnership in rebuilding the team, and for their willingness to allow me to lead them to a new place of respect and honor.

The admin explained that her commitment was only to stay on until a new boss was hired. She appreciated the lunch, but was tired of the snickering and rolling of the eyes from others in the organization, and handed me her official two-week's notice. She wanted to walk away from the disgrace and gossip and had already accepted another position. The training manager said, "Whatever Boss," laughed, but agreed to stay and "give it a go."

I knew I had to rebuild the team up-from-the ashes with a new strategy that didn't resemble the previous structure or mindset. (I wanted to post a big sign outside our area which said "Under New Management," but I thought that might be tacky.)

Assessments

Even as I recruited and hired new staff, we conducted a thorough gap analysis, focusing on "whats and whys": what training was essential and why, what the unmet needs and frustrations were and why they were happening, and what resources were available in our current state.

While my new team worked together collecting data, I met with the executive committee (EC) to gain insight on the organization's needs, and explain how I believed training could significantly impact the business (in a positive way, of course).

A New Direction

My team and I were working so hard and fast trying to keep up with requests for training that we relapsed into reactive patterns—unable to think beyond the moment. We weren't assessing our effectiveness, nor making use of the data we'd pulled together. My new team felt frustrated and unsuccessful. *(Here's an important note: I didn't make any assumptions—I asked them how they were feeling.)* Something had to change, and as leader, I had been tagged "It."

During the following weekly meeting, we agreed that the runaway train had to stop. I looked each one in the eye, and began asking my *what-ifs*:

- What if we "blew up" the existing training norms and started over?
- What if we developed training partners—subject matter experts—to help us deliver training in all areas?
- What if we organized all the existing programs and institutionalized them under one umbrella?
- What if employees got "credit" for training as part of their performance appraisals?
- What if training was so integrated in the organization's business success, and its systems, that to eliminate the training department would be to unravel part of the company's business strategy and culture?
- What if we decided to "just do it"?

The more we talked, the more excited the team became. They looked at each other and laughed with nervous anticipation.

"So?" I said.

And they responded, "Sure. *I'm* in. Let's do it!"

"All right," I announced. "For the next few weeks let's concentrate on changing the paradigm. Our objectives are to recapture training and institutionalize it, make it significant, and make it sustainable. We're going to create a training department that won't burn down!" And with that, we cheered and *high-fived* all around.

The Plan

Our first step was to create a mission and establish a brand. We articulated our reason for being (a mission/purpose) with a value-based identifier that described what we believed about ourselves, and a standard we could be proud of (brand). We knew that if we wanted our stakeholders and clients to see us differently, we first had to see ourselves differently—both individually and collectively.

Next, we created structure. Although we were part of a larger corporation, we decided on the community college model for our training format. Our greatest resource came from the Continuing Education Director at one of our local community colleges, who helped us understand their business and curriculum structure, enrollment process, and marketing strategies. In less than a month we had a plan and a vision.

The team had done their due-diligence: they completed a cost and benefits analysis for making this change and worked out the preliminary logistics for registration and enrollment. We were ready to make our "pitch" to the executive committee.

Buy-in and Partnership

With team members present, I presented our ideas to the committee. It included

- the results of our gap analysis;
- the short and long-term objectives for creating a corporate university solution, including potential barriers;
- the results of the cost and benefits analysis;
- the proposed metrics and success factors;
- what we needed from them to ensure win-win success.

After a lively discussion, we had their buy-in. My team was infused with excitement, confidence, and valued esteem.

Implementation

There was a lot to do, and I asked the team to divide the workload as they deemed fair. I monitored execution and productivity for both results and burn-out, worked side-by-side with team members to teach new skills, secured resources, and removed as many obstacles as possible. I also taught my share of classes to lessen the load on my trainers.

As a group, we identified skill competencies, performance criteria, and expectations for both our potential subject-matter-expert trainers (SMEs) and ourselves. After recruiting and training our new SME faculty, our team of four training managers grew to include seventy-two staff volunteers. We were no longer just a training department; we were a training academy!

Conclusion

Thirty days from the executive committee's "green light," our Academy became reality. From ashes to glory, a team of four individuals, with a dedicated leader-coach, reclaimed the dignity of their department and created partnerships that helped them recover from their catastrophic perfect storm.

Team members were coached on internal politics, business acumen, team dynamics, conflict resolution, facilitation skills, and each earned teaching certifications that allowed our courses to be articulated for college credit.

They changed from being a disjointed, reactionary team of instructors, to an organization of learning professionals and internal business partners. As the team excelled, senior executives assigned high potentials to the team to be groomed for higher positions. We were called "The Farm," and over half our team members became vice presidents and directors.

This is just one example of what can happen with an effective combination of leadership and coaching. After many years of developing my own teams, I now partner with leaders to help coach their teams while becoming, themselves, master leader-coaches.

Let me partner with you and help inspire your team to greatness!

For a free copy of *Motivating Employees During Lean Times* follow this link:

- http://user1584761.sites.myregisteredsite.com/id77.htm

More publications at:

- http://seraphimconsulting.net/id70.html
- Or visit my website: SeraphimConsulting.net

Meet Linda Callecod

Linda Callecod, executive coach and consultant, keynote speaker, author, and master trainer/facilitator, is president of Seraphim Consulting and Training in Federal Way, Washington. She is also the Senior OD Consultant for University of Washington's Professional & Organizational Development department. Linda is a fourteen year veteran instructor for the university's continuing education programs, for which she received their Teaching Excellence Award in business and management. Before 2009, she was divisional vice president of training and diversity for The Bon Marché/Macy's in Seattle.

Linda has over twenty-five years' experience developing leaders and teams across industries and at all levels of an organization. Her specialty is balancing the people side of leadership (emotional intelligence) with the organizational side of business (strategic management) and helping clients create a road map of practical approaches to accomplish individual and organizational results.

Linda's signature brand is her colorful, out-of-the-box creative energy, and her charismatic style. Notwithstanding, her work is based on theoretical soundness, a holistic-systems perspective, and meaningful, quantifiable, action. She delivers highly efficient, yet entertaining and fun learning experiences, with game-changing, achievement focused, coaching.

Leaders and their teams are strengthened, fortified, and aligned through her insight, professional tools, and commitment to excellence. Visit SeraphimConsulting.net.

FOUR

How Rewriting the Golden Rule Changed My Life

By Trisha Harp

Treat others as they want to be treated. And express gratitude in the ways that are meaningful to them. When we operate with these two mantras in mind, amazing changes can occur. This is how we open up the lines of communication without added defenses.

LIKE SO MANY OTHERS, I was taught the Golden Rule when I was growing up. The meaning of "Do unto others as you would have them do unto you" seemed clear enough: treat others as you would want to be treated. So I did. I tried to treat others with the kindness and respect that I sought from others, as the Golden Rule insisted. But after a while, I also noticed a big problem with this popular guiding principle. Often, what I was doing for others didn't match up with what I would want if the situation were reversed. I don't particularly care for Thank You notes and I don't need more trinkets from people, but according to the Golden Rule, that would mean I shouldn't give them to others, either. But the truth is other people really value them.

Sure enough, after over a decade of doing my own proprietary research, collecting data, interviewing people, coaching men, women, and couples, one thing has become crystal clear: the Golden Rule isn't always golden. Quite the opposite. If we really want to give to others, we shouldn't treat them as *we* want to be treated. We should treat them as *they* want to be treated.

I like to call this the Platinum Rule! As individuals, we experience and receive love and appreciation in our own unique ways. What is meaningful to one person might not impact another in the same way. In my research on how marriage and entrepreneurship intertwine, the disconnect that kept cropping up between the couples I researched was due to the fact that they hadn't communicated enough with one another. They had not discussed what they wanted and how they would like to be treated.

Several years ago, my husband started talking to me about one of his companies. I launched in, giving suggestions and trying to solve his issues, but I began to notice that the more I spoke, the less he shared. I realized that I didn't really know what he wanted from me. Did he just want to vent? Or did he want me to be a sounding board for him to think through a dilemma that was facing him? So I asked him, "Do you want my feedback or would you prefer I just listen?" Treat others as *they* want to be treated. At that moment, he just needed an ear he could trust. This was a huge breakthrough for us.

A few years after that, we were working out weekend parenting agreements for our two young children. We had agreed that, on weekends, one of us would take the boys and allow the other to sleep in. Like clockwork, on my husband's mornings, he would get the boys dressed and they'd leave the house together. I assumed he did so because he had trouble entertaining them at home. I was different: on my mornings, I kept the boys occupied at home and away from my husband.

One day, he came to me, somewhat annoyed. "Why don't you take the boys out of the house like I do for you?" he asked. I was surprised. I told him I didn't need him to take the boys out for me. I used earplugs when I was sleeping and their noise didn't bother me. But he couldn't fully relax and fall asleep when the kids were around. Instead, he was trying to lead by example and get me to take the boys out of the house. So we changed our habits and started to give each other what the *other* wanted. There it is again: treat others as *they* want to be treated.

In the movie *Parenthood*, there's a scene with Steve Martin that has stuck with me. He's sitting in the audience, watching his child on stage, and all he can think about is how his life is like a roller coaster. The scene sticks with me because I have often felt like my own life was a lot like a roller coaster ride. I've spent a lot of time wondering if there is anything I can do to ensure that the individuals I hold most dear are still on the ride with me at the end.

Take a moment and think about a roller coaster that you love. One that has twists, turns, upside down parts, and hills that make your stomach drop! Now think about your life. Who is the single most important person you want to share your life's journey with *right now*? It could be a spouse, a parent, a best friend, a sibling, or a child. Imagine that individual sitting next to you in a roller coaster cart. Now imagine you're going up the hill together. Inching up closer and closer to the top. Anxiety and anticipation are escalating. Click after click, you start to wonder if this will be the best roller coaster you've ever experienced. Suddenly your companion puts their hand in front of your eyes and, no matter what you do, they won't remove it.

How do you feel? Angry? Scared? Resentful? Anxious? Frustrated? Will you want to go on another ride with your companion after this experience? Maybe not.

Yet this is exactly how others feel when you don't share with them what you're thinking, feeling, or experiencing in your life. They are essentially riding a roller coaster blind—and they have no clue how to change their circumstances. As a result, the lack of communication creates dissonance between the two of you and robs you of the potential for deeper connection and joy.

I came across a podcast that suggested that one person's failure to *show* gratitude can be felt as *ingratitude* by the other person. I call it the Gratitude Rule! When I look back on my own life, I can see that all those times that I didn't call a friend, write a Thank You note, or buy a trinket, I had no intention to express ingratitude for those people's roles in my life. But if this sentiment is correct, that is what was unintentionally conveyed and I can no longer be surprised that those relationships suffered. By not communicating, I had, in effect, put my hand over their eyes on our roller coaster ride through life together.

After decades of analysis, I have come to this conclusion: by combining the Gratitude Rule with the Platinum Rule, I believe we can enhance our connections and relationships with one another like never before.

In my seminars and coaching sessions, I give the following exercise: choose two people in your personal life and two people at work. Then, ask those individuals to write down four things that you can do to show them how much they mean to you or how much you appreciate them. Then commit to doing those four things over the next month or two. After two months have passed, ask them how your actions made them feel and if they have any new suggestions for you. From this, you'll gain valuable insight into how those around you want to be treated and how they receive acts of appreciation. And you'll also be showing gratitude in the ways that mean the most to them.

Yet some people feel that it's less meaningful for them if they have to ask someone for what they want, rather than the other person figuring it out on their own. If that's you, think of it this way: if something is meaningful enough to you, it will feel wonderful no matter what, even if you had to ask for it.

That said, *how* you ask also matters. It's best to come from a place of love and genuineness. Your words should not be dripping with bitterness, doubt, or contention. For example, perhaps you'd like to get some help with the laundry on a regular basis. It could easily backfire if you have attitude when you ask, "I wonder if you could help with the laundry once in a while so I don't *always* have to do it." Instead, try, "You know, the part about doing the laundry that I dislike the most is _____. Could you start helping me with that? It would really make me happy and would help a lot." Part of what makes the Platinum Rule work so well is that it gives you a lot of latitude to be specific about exactly what you want or need to be happier. The more specific you are, the more those around you will know what to do to make you happy.

But what if you don't know what you want? Trial and error is a wonderful thing. We are all dynamic human beings and change our minds regularly. If something doesn't work or stops working for you, let the other person know. Say something like, "You know how I thought _____ would help with the laundry? Actually, that didn't seem to make a difference. Can we try _____ instead? Thank you!"

Treat others as *they* want to be treated. And express gratitude in the ways that are meaningful to *them*. When we operate with these two mantras in mind, amazing changes can occur. This is how we open up the lines of communication without added defenses.

How does the Platinum Rule and the Gratitude Rule apply at your work place? Research shows that when a business incorporates a value-based recognition system—a program that specifies ways to show appreciation for its employees' work and contributions— there is less turnover, higher employee engagement, and an increase in the bottom line. In addition to my coaching and seminars, I work with many companies to help them build rapport within the organization using the very same methods I've been discussing in this chapter.

Aim to make communication and appreciation simple and habitual. Eventually, you will naturally do things for those around you because you know what makes them happy. And hopefully, they will return the favor.

My hope for you is to increase your "bottom line" both at home and at your office by becoming more aware of how those in your life want to be treated—and then acting on that awareness. If you would like to receive a free PDF of my book, "Me | You: A 52-Week Guide Toward Making *Appreciation* Simple and Habitual," email me at Trisha.Harp@HarpFamilyInstitute.com.

Meet Trisha Harp

Trisha Harp, M.S., C.P.C., is an entrepreneur, researcher, author, and coach. She is no stranger to the entrepreneurial household. Not only was she born into one, she and her husband have created several companies of their own together. Trisha founded the Harp Family Institute and has worked with entrepreneurs for the past fifteen years. She and her husband have successfully integrated their personal and business lives and have discovered how to strengthen their relationship and optimize their communication.

She has been featured in *Inc. Magazine*, Entrepreneur.com, *The Wall Street Journal*, and Forbes.com. To learn more about Trisha and her work, visit HarpFamilyInstitute.com.

FIVE

A Professional Approach to Success

THE POWER OF COACHING

By Jason Arispe

Leaders of the past knew how to tell. Leaders of the future must know how to elicit best thinking and decision making and make sure everyone in their organization can do the same.
That's coaching.

COACHING IS a process that allows people to take charge of their challenges in personally tailored ways, ultimately leading them towards happier, healthier, and more productive lives.

Coaching as a vehicle is a conveyance by which people can move from where they are to where they wanted to be. Its first practitioners understood that the key to coaching's success in facilitating personal change was a skillful conversation that incited better and expanded thinking. Both the coaching conversation and the new learning it generated were understood to be the conveyance, not the expertise and knowledge of the coaches themselves. However, as coaching began to catch on with the general public, its meaning was popularized and changed. When I say I am a professional coach, some people say, "I coach," most people ask, "What sport?" Today the word "coach" is used indiscriminately, and the focus has switched from skillful conversation that incites best thinking to the experience of the person doing the coaching. We have "career coaches," "business coaches," and even "relationship coaches." But what we don't have today is a way to immediately tell whether the "sales coach" is skilled at coaching or skilled at sales. Indeed, the word "coach" is on the verge of losing any dependable meaning, and if the term is not demystified soon, we will be in danger of obscuring coaching's proven benefits and removing it from the serious consideration of wellness practitioners.

To preserve the rigor that Certified Professional Coaching brings, let's take a look at some benchmarks that identify professional coaching, allowing us as professional coaches to distinguish it from other models of the same name. Coaching is different from mentoring, consulting, teaching, and advice giving. Coaching is conversation that elicits best thinking and decision making so people can create results that are important to them.

Through the conversation led by great coaching questions, people expand their thinking about important changes and ways to accomplish them. Generating new and expanded thinking is why it's important that the coaching process allows people to answer these questions for themselves. Coaching allows people to work toward goals that are important to them and take charge of their challenges in personally tailored ways, increasing their ability to accomplish additional changes on their own in the future and ultimately leading toward happier, healthier, and more satisfying and productive lives.

If the purpose of coaching is to elicit best thinking and decision making, it follows that less and less coaching will be needed over time.

Coaching builds capability in people that outlasts the coach and reduces the need for ongoing coaching. To accomplish this desired result, coaching approaches should share four goals:

- Creation and management of mutual trust
- Facilitation of best thinking and decision making
- Development of both autonomy and interdependence
- Increased capacity for thinking more expansively and at higher levels

Coaching relationships that begin and end with these four goals result in more effective decision making, problem solving, and self-initiated continuous learning. When this occurs, the benefits of coaching outlast the coach. This is the goal of coaching.

Coaching has absolute standards you can count on and without a strong foundation, standards are words without substance. When an effective definition of coaching is in place, presuppositions that improve performance are practiced, and goals to increase independent capacity should be established:

- Coaching is always a product of caring relationships.
- Coaching always gets results.
- Coaching is never destructive.
- Coaching aims for the best that can be achieved and never settles for less.
- Coaching always remains alert for improvement.
- Coaching never tells people what to do.
- Coaching will always seem right; if it doesn't seem right, it's not.

- Coaching builds capability, never dependency.

By now you may be thinking, *Ok, I see the differences between coaching and mentoring, consulting, teaching, and advice giving. But is it really effective? Can it really work for me?* Let me tell you, yes it is effective and you can benefit from being coached!

Let's talk about a few myths regarding coaching:

Myth #1: You Can't Define Coaching.

This is false. In fact, if coaching can't be defined, how can you know it's coaching? The reality is that coaching has a solid definition you can depend on. Coaching is conversation that elicits best thinking and decision making so people can create results that are important to them.

Myth #2: Coaching Is Managing with a Happy Face.

When people don't make important lifestyle changes, a manager can feel that smiling is the best way to keep the subject open. That's because managing is making sure people do what they're supposed to do. Sometimes it works, but, too often, the benefits of successful management leave with the manager. Coaching isn't managing. Coaching is making sure people's internal capacity to produce results on their own increases over time. With coaching, the benefits outlast the coach.

Myth #3: Coaching Is Just Another Name for Mentoring.

A mentor "knows the ropes," provides guidance, shares his or her experience, and passes on lessons learned. That's mentoring, and it's great and has its place in personal development; it's just not coaching. When someone refers to their work as "coaching" and then uses the word interchangeably with mentoring, consulting, teaching, and advice giving, expect that you might benefit but don't expect to get coaching.

Myth #4: Being a Coach Means Being a Cheerleader.

Getting people to feel fired up and motivated about living a healthy lifestyle is great and has a place in any organization. However, it's no secret the results of cheerleading are limited; the feeling goes away and it's back to business as usual. Coaching is about continuous support in eliciting best thinking and decision making toward taking action that produces sustainable results. With coaching, the expectation is that cheering is reserved for accomplished goals and actions that occur along the way.

Myth #5: Coaching Takes Too Long.

It might seem quicker to tell someone what they ought to do. If information and advice resulted in healthy lifestyles, we'd all live to 120 and bicycle/swim and eat well to the end. Those who experience true coaching find that it actually saves time because people are more likely to do what they, themselves, figure out is right for their lives. Additionally, eliciting and expanding best thinking through coaching increases people's capacity to think better on their own. Over time, this adds up. Coaching respects processes, expects results, and takes only the time that is necessary.

Myth #6: Coaching Is a Kind of Psychotherapy.

While coaching requires a fundamental knowledge of how people best achieve their goals, it does not focus on a person's psychological history. In therapy, people expect to focus on the impact of past experiences on present difficulties. With coaching, people should expect to look at what to do now to take charge of the present and future.

Myth #7: One Recipe Can Handle All Coaching Situations.

It's not unusual to see a health education program called coaching. That's a mistake. Coaching is not a one-size-fits-all activity, and no single program does what coaching does. How people best determine and achieve wellness goals is highly varied; wellness programs, alone, aren't customized enough to get the job done well. Integrate them with coaching and watch the results soar.

Myth #8: I Just Can't Be Coached.

People who are unresponsive to coaching are too often labeled uncoachable. Sure, sometimes what is needed is a doctor instead of a coach. However, when someone is unresponsive to coaching, it's usually more productive to find out what's holding the person back instead of labeling him or her as a problem. Often what's needed is simply a clarification of goals or a different coach.

Myth #9: If You Successfully Coach People, They May Leave.

Sometimes people will find out they are working at the wrong job and, in that case, you want to find out sooner rather than later. Sometimes people will make lifestyle changes that temporarily disrupt things at work. However, more often, people being coached will find out more about what they bring to the table both at work and to their lives in general. They get jazzed about it and feel greater loyalty because their organization is helping them reveal, reach for, and utilize their full potential.

Myth #10: Coaching Doesn't Add to the Bottom Line.

People get that impression because they think coaching is just another version of more of the same. And, if they fall for any of the above myths, more of the same is what they will get. Coaching isn't just another program; it's different. It builds consistent, replicable results because it's a science that develops people to think more effectively about accomplishing results that are impor-tant to them. High Quality Coaching generates self-assessment, responsibility taking, and leadership thinking. Over time, that has a substantial impact on any organization's bottom line.

As you can see Coaching is an established, structured, meaningful, and professional approach to success. Perhaps like many of my clients, you are on the road to success and have stopped at the 24 hour diner and haven't left. Are you still there enjoying another cup of coffee and a slice of homemade pie, living off your past successes…?

If the answer is yes, it's time to get back on the road! Perhaps you forgot what direction you were going or you need a new direction entirely.

Coaching can help! Coaching can open doors that find answers, not pre-packaged answers that don't fit, but answers that help you meet your "saboteurs" face to face.

Meet Jason Arispe

Jason Arispe, a professional with over 20 years of experience in fields ranging from HR, Healthcare, Insurance, Marketing and Advertising and IT is here to "Help You Find Your Synergies for Success."

Jason's diverse background has afforded him the opportunity to collaborate globally. Companies such as AOL, IBM, US Military, Volvo, and Toshiba have utilized his skills to develop systems, programs, and plans of action.

He has successfully started private and non-profit companies and is now pursuing lifelong work with those who have a vision for an extraordinary quality of life, are seeking to reach personal or professional goals, or wish to create optimal balance in their lives.

Jason is passionate about empowering you to synergize your own strengths, desires, and passions so that you can overcome obstacles and take the necessary steps to achieve your dreams and goals.

Jason states; "If I can give you two things, they will be insight and empowerment. When I'm not focusing on coaching, I'm with my family. Being a husband and a father is perhaps my most significant qualification. My children put me to the test daily, constantly testing the authenticity of the methods I use with my clients."

jasonarispe.com

SIX

Cross Cultural Business Coaching at the Highest Level

RELATIONSHIP IS KEY

By Helen Yu-Hua Chu

ONCE, when I was about ten years old, an elderly couple had come to visit my father. I was sitting at their feet pouring tea, as befitting a proper Chinese daughter. This couple had invested their hard-earned savings with a stock broker, but unfortunately the broker had given them bad advice and they had lost their investment. Sometime later, this couple decided to invest with the same broker again. The broker again managed to lose their investment. After a few years, the couple had sold their house and brought their last savings to this same broker to invest. Sure enough, the broker lost it all!

Upon hearing their story, my father asked the couple why they kept investing their life's savings with this broker after so many failures.

The old man said, "We figure he had bad luck in those few years, poor guy. We thought maybe he would not be that unlucky...after all, he lost two times already. The third time should be a charm! Well, I guessed wrong. He REALLY had bad luck! Poor man!"

At that time, I had the following thoughts:

1. This poor couple was conned!
2. I need to learn how to avoid this type of incompetence or thievery.
3. I need to help others so they don't suffer the same fate.
4. I need to have the best possible relationship with everyone I work with, so they will overlook my flaws.

Knowledge + Integrity = Credibility

In order to establish a close relationship with one's clients, one must first understand their background and their likes and dislikes. One should seek to respect their clients from the bottom of their heart. Many people think that a superficially well-mannered business style is good enough. They do not understand that sensitive clients can tell a genuinely friendly business person who respects their cultural background from one who is outwardly well-mannered but inwardly arrogant or disrespectful.

The higher the ranking or wealth of the clients, the more sensitive they will be! These people have generally acquired their wealth and status through hard work and experience. Even if they were born into "old money," they would have been trained to watch out for con men and people who would take advantage of them. Otherwise, they would have lost most of their money long before they met you. By the time they meet with you, they probably have learned all the key words, phrases, and tactics that most con men would do or say. Anything you do or say, they can see through you.

Try to be honest and sincere. Try to be understanding of their busy schedule and overcrowded personal space. Treat them with respect, but with self-confidence. If you have a service or a business idea to bring to their attention, they will either think you are great or think you are an idiot! What is to lose? You have a 50/50 opportunity to gain their support. The best way to approach these clients is to present your proposal in a prepared and confident manner. As long as you do your homework right and you don't screw up your presentation, you will have a better chance to win your clients over.

Finding Common Ground

Part of the process of starting a relationship with your clients is to establish some initial common ground that you both can relate to. Paying attention to different aspects of their lives is a must. What does your client like? What is your client's background? Does he/she have family members? Does he/she have children? Where and how does he/she like to spend his/her leisure time? Does he/she have certain hobbies?

The key is to engage in what your clients like and to at least have some knowledge about the areas your clients are interested in. Always have a few topics other than business to lead into deeper conversation, to let your clients know you as a person, or better yet, to know you as a friend or a fellow enthusiast of a certain hobby or a certain entertainment.

Kindness + Respect + Sincerity = Trust

One item I would like to remind you: NOT EVERYONE likes the entertainment/dining activities that you are into. When you are working on a business deal with someone from another geographic location or cultural background, you must take extra care. They might not like to go to the bars after work. They might not like to talk about American football, nor care about certain famous local sports figures. They might not like to smoke or drink, or enjoy loud music. They might feel uncomfortable in a Las Vegas setting. Worse yet, they might not like your cheese and wine party!

When my family first arrived in Los Angeles from Taiwan, our Real Estate Broker—Marilyn—invited us to a cocktail party. Expecting to find an assortment of appetizers and hot foods, we instead encountered a very typical American cheese and wine party. There is a book written by Fred Schneiter about the attempt to bring certain western foods to China. The average Chinese person's disgust for cheese could be summarized by one of the book's chapters: "Chinese Mice Don't Eat Cheese!" Our family could stomach neither the cheese nor the wine, and departed early. Since my mother was one of her bigger investors and my father was the one paying the bills, Marilyn had made a very big mistake.

Fortunately, Marilyn had already established herself with my mother as a kind and caring friend. She had not looked down on my mother who barely spoke English. Nor did she lose patience when my mom asked the same questions over and over again. She knew my mother did not understand some of the processes of purchasing real estate in the U.S.

So in the end, our family simply ignored the wine and cheese incident and bought a very nice four unit apartment right across from the Los Alamitos race track during a time of peak interest rates—a situation highly beneficial to Marilyn.

Myth of the Home Court Advantage

In Asia and other old world cultures, many seemingly unsophisticated people may actually be shrewd business persons. They learned from their environments of the old world economy, and they would not dare to leave home and the familiar environment if they were not at least brave enough and smart enough to be able to handle many situations that could cost their money or even their life.

Although Marilyn the realtor had earned my mother's trust, she probably never suspected that my mother was continually testing her. Having survived a war torn life in China, and having set up her own clothing business in Taiwan, my mother was not only a smart business woman, she was very streetwise—and tough as nails. My mother may not have known English and been well educated, but she was always prepared to catch Marilyn if she was inconsistent in her responses to my mother's questions.

Never underestimate someone from a foreign culture. And never assume that the one who does most of the talking has the advantage—it is usually the opposite.

Navigating the Cultural Divide

In each culture there are different rules. For example, most Eastern Asian families that were influenced by the philosophy of Confucius have one thing in common: women are the ones who control the family purse strings. When I started my married life with my husband in America, it was common for American salesmen to attempt to sidestep me and talk to my husband about financial matters, such as purchasing life insurance, property insurance, estate planning, and financial planning. Generally, businesswomen would not make the same mistake.

While working in the high tech industry, I would sometimes observe similar behavior on the part of my bosses—not only in how they treated myself, but in how they treated their customers. Ironically, I would often be placed in the role of rekindling a better relationship with our clients after the damage had already been done. After experiencing enough repetitions of this pattern, I decided I would start my own Business Consulting/Coaching firm to hopefully help others to NOT make those same mistakes.

Being born to one of the top Chinese Business traditions, the Zhejiang Merchants—and with my father being a high powered International Corporate and Estate Lawyer, and my mother being an innovative businesswoman, I have witnessed firsthand the many day to day issues and pitfalls both in international corporations as well as small ma and pa shops. Throughout my life both in Taiwan and the U.S.—as well as China, I was surrounded by cousins, friends, and close acquaintances who were steeped in the business world. Some of them were CEOs of international corporations. Some of them operated local mom and pop shops. Some were not directly involved in their own business, but were policy makers who regularly made decisions that impacted businessmen big and small. And so my upbringing was steeped in the wisdom, interactions, and mentoring of these people.

I believe I am very qualified to coach interested people who want to do business cross culturally. Whether you are an Asian businessperson wanting to do business in the West and not understanding how to go about it, or you are an American/European wanting to do business in Asia and could not understand the 99 different ways Asians say NO, my services are critical to your success.

We Americans often think the world is very small and everyone has a common ground for understanding. But the truth is much more complex. And we should always be prepared when we seek to do business with people from other places and other cultures.

Meet Helen Yu-Hua Chu

Born into a scholarly family with deep-rooted traditions, Helen Yu-Hua Chu was mentored early on by some of the top political

and business leaders who helped shape modern China. She attended a prep school with elite children of Taiwan's high society, then transferred to the United States, and graduated with a Bachelor's degree from the School of Information and Computer Science at UC Irvine. Working approximately twenty years in Southern California's high tech industry, Helen's career focused on combining innovative technology with business process engineering solutions for a wide selection of clients, including GE Supply, Walmart, Sam's Club, Hudson's Bay Company of Canada, DHL, and United Airlines. Helen has been invited to engagements in New York, Shanghai, Hong Kong, and Bangkok to train and present papers to engineers and corporate management on the process of system engineering and proper business practices in the modern high tech world.

Contact Information:

- Phone: 949- 329-8391
- Email: HelenChu@CoachForYou.org
- Website: CoachForYou.org

SEVEN

Love Beyond Fear

By Johanna Jobin

Did you know that unlimited potential sleeps inside of you? You wonder if life has anything else to offer you? Yes, you finally have the opportunity to rewrite the story of your life and make decisions based on your true values while being freed from your blockages, beliefs, and the fear of what others think. We must rewrite our life from point Zero. This chapter is offered to help you participate more conscientiously in your release of what holds you back. You must already be well aware of human duality, to open your mind to reality. In this chapter, you will find various steps in the journey of a person seeking a better quality of life. Each stage carries internal mutations.

Live It from the Heart

See how balance occurs naturally when we trust our heart. See how much easier life can be when we live it from the heart.

A CALL for Help

Fear is created as soon as we are in the fetus and when we are born. The memories of the energies of each moment creates either a blockage or love. And here starts life, learning to manage our emotions and our false beliefs.

It all started the day Jacynthe called for help. She felt lost, she was sad and confused. She was taking anti-depression medication. Everything was scary, she didn't know where she was standing anymore. She had lost all hope and was totally desperate.

That day, Jacynthe heard her inner voice, and life guided her to stop associating asking for help with being weak or failing. Through grapevines she found me and decided to transform her daily life with a life coach.

While on the phone with her, I quickly felt the urgency of the crisis she was in. Her vibration was very low, she was caught in a web of sufferance, fears, beliefs, and illusions. She said, "I need help, I can't go lower, I'm ready for peace." She seriously wanted to free herself from the chains of her past.

Greeting the Changes

After explaining the process of the journey, she was just about to start, Jacynthe at the end of her roll and in full depression, accepted to live the changes of new perspectives. Getting her ready for big revelations coming to her in a private personal way level, even if it's disruptive it will help and serve her in this life. She finally understood how a Life Coach could help her. It's a go, she decides to hire me, to trust me, and to fully welcome and greet the changes that await her.

To start, she had to learn to communicate with herself before anyone else. She began to take sacred time to think about the life she wanted. After realizing that she was living totally the opposite, she begins to pull herself together.

I decide to show her the Point Zero technique that I developed during my quest. It really started to change her totally. She lost weight. She ate better. She perceived her family and friends a total different way. She started to embrace everyone she pushed away. She's now embracing the simple things that bring her joy. A huge wake up call, my coaching technique keeps her calm despite the chaos around her.

Establishing a Harmonious Relationship

Once Jacynthe realized she couldn't really make it through this life alone, I became her support system. It was time to undertake the discovery of a harmonious relationship with herself. With a commitment to choose to surround herself with people and harmonious things.

She embraces the Point Zero technique and it is working, she is connected to her soul. She can now reclaim her personal power, discover her true being, her potential.

Joy is making surface. With practice, she finds new ways to create, to live fully and to love.

Her self-esteem is now born, which leads her to develop her authenticity. She starts to understand how to respect herself and her emotions. She now can say that she is physically, mentally, and emotionally connected. Overcoming fears is to choose to put Love beyond.

Developing Authenticity

I'm not talking about ethics here, I'm talking about respecting yourself and falling in love with yourself. Opening to the joy of life, discovering your life mission, regaining your personal power, managing your time and stress. With the help of spiritual laws. Respect for oneself leads to respect for others.

Moment of Pure Harmony

As she is creating her new life, she realizes that there are seasons and cycles in us, just as there are in nature. To learn to recognize and honor the seasons and cycles of the soul, she needs to be in turn listening to vibrations of sounds that bring peace, harmonization, and greater serenity. She let the sounds and their vibrations rock each cell of her body to be touched by the sounds, allowing to raise her vibrations. After a few months, I exposed her to use positive and high-frequency power words, sounds, and people to transform her. And I asked her to trust the magic of her spirit to lead and explore her hidden powers.

The Power of Words and Sacred Songs

The step of understanding that you become what you choose to see, hear, and feel was a big challenge. She learned that all words and sounds contain vibrations and will act directly on her subtle bodies and participate in the openness necessary to accommodate the changes in her life. Not to feed the doubts that may come to visit her. But, to focus on creating her life, the life she wants. She learned to be selective in all her choices, she knows now, she is totally responsible of creating herself.

The Joy of Being Connected

She no longer had to be isolated or suffer from separateness. She takes time to see and honor her connections and value her place in the whole. She learned to be part of a dance, the magical dance of the universe taking place each moment in time. She realized the more she is connected to her soul, the more she counts her blessings, not her loss.

Success in Love

Finally, she understands the different forms of love. That the soul-mate starts with her inner self. To simply succeed in love is to love one another and to respect oneself above all. Love is being realized, created, and to reach beyond your limits. To love an animal is a very good way to understand responsibility and unconditional love. To be of service is a beautiful form of love. First, serve God before all and that starts with gratitude.

I hope this chapter inspired you to want to connect with yourself. Be ready to let go of what does not serve you anymore, so you can get new opportunity flows.

I will always remember when I was totally in despair and didn't know where to begin. The roads diverged in a wood, and I took the one less travelled by, and that has made all the difference. That was gratitude. Knowing that each interaction creates a ripple effect and each encounter helps shape destiny.

I have developed the Point Zero Transformation Program that will change your life forever. It's a perfect way to start your new life. I'm here to serve and support others in their journey to success. Whether it is for a private lesson, a need for deeper understanding, or a spiritual accompaniment, a meeting will help you see the situations from another angle.

I will make sure to show you how to honor your connections and the impact of each person you've met. To see how people have helped shape you and how you've touched and helped shape others. I will take you outside of your old way of thinking—into new territory and possibilities!

Each encounter will allow you to connect and take one step closer to the inner peace that only a deeper understanding can bring. It is a private lesson, an accompaniment adapted to your life!

Real success also includes health, energy, love of life, harmony of relationships, freedom to create, emotional and psychological stability, well-being and peace of mind. And yet all these joys will not satisfy us if we do not cultivate the seeds of the divinity....Succeeding means to meet the divine, wherever we go and in all that surrounds us, in the eyes of a child, the beauty of a flower, the flight of a bird.

A TEACHER TAKES A HAND, OPENS THE MIND, AND TOUCHES THE HEART!

Ask for help and breathe again. Let's change your life forever!

If you would like to get a FREE copy of **The Get Unstuck Now Transformation Form**, go to johannajobincoaching.com. There are 37 awesome questions guaranteed to shake up your thinking, get you unstuck, and moving forward. I highly encourage you to give them a try yourself on any problem you are facing.

Meet Johanna Jobin

Johanna Jobin is a teacher, yoga instructor, certified personal trainer, hypnotherapist, life purpose, recovery coach, and the last but not least Warrior ambassador of light and peace.

As a single mother, she discovers her own global potential through gratitude, self-love, and the courage to be herself. She spoke at the Women Awareness Congress, Virginia Department of Education. She is a self-proclaimed personal development ambassador who has changed her own life. She believes that everyone has a sacred path and once they connect with their soul, their own potential, they too can change their life.

Her quest leads her to use the power of her inner voice that revealed extraordinary tools for all aspects of life. Her education and persevering journey enabled her to acquire an innovative technique to achieve and maintain a state of happiness and inner well-being.

Thanks to her great knowledge of the Soul and the human being, Johanna Jobin accompanies and teaches to disentangle the situations and then take a wise look with the eyes of the Soul.

If you would like to get a FREE copy of **The Warrior Ambassador of Light and Peace Transformation Prayer**, go to johannajobin-coaching.com.

EIGHT

Shame of Love

By Jenn Veal

As life kept moving, I kept moving.
As life unfolded, I evolved.

WHY IS THERE ALWAYS that moment, event, or person that pushes the domino in your chain? The links that change your thinking, your decisions, and your path. Why do those factors make such a huge impact on you, good or bad, whether you know it, don't know it, or until you figure it all out? I look back at who I was, who I became and who I have become. I was a little girl, a blank slate, who became a teenager—"I thought I knew everything but I didn't"—then meshed into "I know it all, but I've been burnt a few too many times" young adult to finally, ME.

As life kept moving, I kept moving. As life unfolded, I evolved.

Growing up in my culture there was an aura of respect we had for our parents and elders no matter what. We did what they said and followed the path they paved for us otherwise it was shameful. I refer to this as the "shame of love." My parents didn't verbally say they loved me or hug me all the time, only during those special occasions or bad events and even then, it was a hit or miss. I just knew they did because they worked so hard to provide a good life for me, a roof over my head, food on the table, clothes on my back, and the best schools. They did what they were supposed to do and I did what was expected of me.

I love my family. I have great early childhood memories of all the fun family parties we attended. It seemed like every weekend someone was celebrating something which meant an all-night, all you can eat huge layout of food, drinks, and *chismis* (small talk, boasting, gossip). Family parties also meant that the adults entertained themselves by playing our cultural game of mahjong, (it's not gambling if you don't play for money, *wink*). My parents would play from the time we arrived to the early morning. There were always a lot of us at these parties, my family, extended family, and close friends.

My parents, like many, have good intentions towards their children. They tried to keep us away from all the "bad" stuff they tell us to stay away from. Not knowing they are the ones that initially exposed us to it in the first place, at no fault to them, they were just enjoying life and we didn't live in a bubble.

My first domino stands here. I was molested as a child by two adult family friends, multiple times at different gatherings. They said I was pretty. They said it was a secret, so it was. I didn't say anything. I didn't want to feel shameful. So, I kept "my secret." I made myself forget (so I thought) and life carried on.

As a teenager, I did what I "felt" was best for me, I had the "experience" to know what was best for me—NOT. Like most teenagers, I rebelled, I made bad decisions, and the consequences that followed changed my path. Running away, gangs, and teen pregnancy back then were just starting to rise up and I became a statistic.

Inevitably, I became the "shame of love" to my family. I was pregnant at sixteen, my senior year of high school. I graduated, had a baby shower instead of my birthday, and became a mother all in the same year. Heartbroken inside, I was not going to show it.

Life, my roller coaster, kept going and so did I. As a young adult, I found myself making "feel good" decisions repeatedly and encountering similar situations after another. I learned through trial and error to get myself back on track as many times as I fell off. I figured out how to survive. I figured out how to maneuver the system to get what I wanted. When others left my side, I found a way. I became resourceful, creative and my own problem solver. I was relentless and was not going to give up. I couldn't, I had a son I had to face every night. I completed LVN school at the age of twenty. I was adamant to prove myself to everyone, especially my family.

For quite some time now, I had been away from home. I started working on my career as a Registered Nurse. I was moving forward in life but inside I wasn't. I was still struggling. I felt inadequate. I was searching for something. I was too prideful to seek help, so instead, I completed a life coaching program to help myself find what I was missing. Things were beginning to come together.

By this time, my family was finally proud of me. I remember the day my dad called me and for the first time, he said, "I'm proud of you, I love you very much," and complimented me on how strong of a woman I had become.

I told him with a big proud smile, "I love you too." We chit chatted for a little because my duties as a mom took over (by this time, I had four angels). As I got off the phone, I felt so accomplished. I had proven myself to my dad. *I did it, unconditional acceptance and love.* I felt so great knowing my dad was proud of me, loved me, and he said it to me. I couldn't wait to plan my big wedding, future trips home for the holidays, and family vacations.

A week later, life threw a gigantic boulder at me. I received a phone call from my brother, "Dad passed away in his sleep." Everything changed.

Life doesn't discriminate. I flew back home, buried my dad, and life didn't stop. My everyday task felt heavier and I felt emptier. Situations, decisions, and consequences continued to pile up as life kept going.

I was depressed. I felt defeated and alone. My relationship was falling apart. I found out I was pregnant again. I was dealing with the death of my dad. I had to help my mom financially survive while surviving myself. I was in serious debt. I was losing my home. Everything was wrong. Everything was upside down and I couldn't turn it around. My normal, my comfort was no longer my accomplishments but my daily cry in the shower. I felt failure.

The day came and I gave birth to my son. I had complications during pregnancy because of all the turmoil I was going through. He had complications after birth and stayed in the hospital a few days longer. I didn't leave, I was not going home without him. I slept in the visitor's lounge and stayed with him as much as the nurses allowed. I prayed. I promised. "God please help my son." He eventually was discharged home and the joy of him gave me hope again. God sent me another angel.

Just as I thought everything was settling, life continued. "My secret" caught up with me. I no longer was that little girl. I was becoming ME. I found myself asking God again to help me but this time I was on my knees with tears rolling down my face, shamed and exhausted. "God please help me. I have nothing else to give but me." I let go and my dominoes fell.

Everyone has a limit. I reached mine. It was hard for me to ask for help. I was afraid. I was doing everything myself for so long—seconds, minutes, hours, became days, weeks, months, and years. I got used to pushing through all my daily duties as a mom and all the other titles I carried. Only I knew, I felt lost, fearful, inferior, and not enough. I excelled on the outside only to cover the inside. I held onto the person everyone expected me to be and ignored ME. I was consumed to the point I forgot me. I forgot to love me, forgive me and care for me. I was so lost within myself. I was blinded. I lost who I really was, who I wanted to be, and where I wanted my life to go.

You see, my life is a series of events and lessons. Events that are triggered one after the other. Lessons I learned from trial and error. As life unfolded, I evolved. I decided to leverage my skills, abilities, and experiences to help others, as a nurse, as a case manager, as a life coach. I added a few other accolades to my name but this one was for me, Life RESET Strategist.

It took these chains of events to push me into my destiny.

I am who I am because of my past, my present, and the future I am creating. Life didn't change. I did. Without these events, I would not be who I have become today. The key is to continue to evolve, be brave in the truth, seek help, learn, and find encouragement along the way.

I share my story to give hope to those struggling to release who they were, who they are, and who they're fighting to become.

My favorite quote:

You may encounter many defeats, but you must not be defeated. In fact, it may be necessary to encounter the defeats, so you can know who you are, what you can rise from, how you can still come out of it.

- Maya Angelou

Meet Jenn Veal

Jenn Veal is a Life RESET Strategist, a Registered Nurse for over twenty years specializing in Case Management, Creator of the RESET it! and PUSH it! Buttons, a Real Estate Broker, Business Owner, Author and an Entrepreneur.

Jenn created a way to level up in life and now helps others do just that. Jenn found herself having to problem solve, strategize, and design her own diagram to success throughout her personal life, career, and spiritual journey regardless of her circumstances. Her knowledge as a Registered Nurse and skills as a Case Manager gives her the added advantage as a Life RESET Strategist. Jenn mentors individuals who are ready to RESET their direction to their destiny. She provides the support, accountability, and personalized action steps to move forward. Jenn states, "It's my joy witnessing my clients succeed, and in return, my clients helping others succeed."

Jenn is married, has five children, three grandchildren, and two dogs. She loves spending time with her family and creating life-time memories. Jenn Veal is a Game Changer!

SHARE YOUR STORY. Ask Jenn questions. She would love to hear from you, encourage you and help you RESET it!

For support and guidance through your journey contact Jenn at 1-866-773-3133, email JennVeal@outlook.com, and visit PushbyJenn.com

NINE

Coming Home

TRANSFORM LOW SELF-ESTEEM INTO SELF LOVE–
KNOWING THE DIFFERENCE BETWEEN POWER
AND FORCE

By Matthew J. Moody

BEFORE I COULD BEGIN to help people, I needed to reflect on my past and find a way to love myself fully. My family knew I was bright and would tell me so. Why was that so hard for me to believe? I was the last to believe it. In many ways, being told I was wonderful, and a gift from God, gave me a life pass to learn and love, and to leave home to begin my journey and explore the world. As a teen, I knew was gay and while my family accepted me, there was a pervading sense of disappointment projected by my family, counselors, and others in my community. I had to leave home to discover my true self and reclaim my self-esteem. At eighteen years old, I found myself transplanted from the rural cowboy and country life of Colorado to living in Mission Beach in San Diego, where I was full of myself, my ideas, yet still a child in many ways, and almost always afraid. Being afraid, or numbing the pain was always in the back of my mind and life.

Although I stayed for only a year, it was long enough to know that I would love California the rest of my life, and have a foothold and heart along the West Coast. I didn't know what to study, but I knew it was time to figure it out. I moved back to Colorado and became a hairdresser. I was told by someone I loved and trusted that because I was gay hairdressing was something I could do. This was a bittersweet, narrow-minded perception that turned out to be a gift, as I try to make everything in my life. Through this very social profession I was introduced to a wealth of lessons that are still priceless.

I moved to Santa Fe, New Mexico, a couple of years later and began to heal and grow. My path over the next twenty-five years as a hairdresser led to my owning multiple salons and spas. At the time, I hadn't gone to college and became quite successful, yet still had a vein of low self-esteem and was always trying to force and forge ahead. I did not understand yet the difference between power, which is eternally energizing and supportive, and force, which comes from my ego and eventually ends in exhausting the energy. I matured during those years, through a series of challenging relationships, and a lot of work on myself. Santa Fe (The City of Holy Faith, or in the long translation of Santa Fe, *La Villa Real de la Santa Fe de San Francisco de Asís*, the Royal Town of the Holy Faith of Saint Francis of Assisi) is an amazing place to be healed and put through one's paces.

I had the fortune to know a very eclectic group of clients, many of whom are still my teachers and friends. I've had the good fortune to meet many of the world's most famous mystics, gurus, teachers, politicians (from presidential to local), movie stars, authors, and philanthropists. I have also been blessed not to be superficially impressed by these people. Every one of them helped me heal my low self-esteem, and move forward. During this time, I felt it was time to do something service-oriented with my talents. I became a Nationally Registered Emergency Medical Technician (NREMT) and a firefighter on an Indian reservation near Santa Fe, as well as a volunteer support buddy for New Mexico AIDS Services.

At the same time, I founded Heartbridge, a nonprofit that helped people in a serious health or spiritual crisis. Heartbridge led me to the University of New Mexico's Anderson School of Business for a certification in nonprofit administration, where I began to practice philanthropy and began to mature. I explored various spiritual practices and studied with Joan Halifax and UPAYA where she founded her Being with Dying program. I ended up taking my precept training under Roshi Joan and through her, Thich Naht Hahn. My dharma name is Jewel of the Source.

I ran Heartbridge for twelve years. Heartbridge provided support for people nationwide with cancer and serious physical disfigurement. I closed Heartbridge when it was time to move into coaching and when the mission felt filled. Hairdressing, spiritual exploration, and Heartbridge made fertile ground for what I practice today.

I went back to school, became a real estate broker and personal coach, and began to coach. This path began partly because of my life scars related to my life path, and the desire to make my family proud of me. I continued to study and furthered my personal development. In 2004, my real estate business helped me to leave the fashion and hair business. I maintain a real estate brokerage and referring consulting practice today.

When the last recession occurred in the United States (and abroad) my friend and real estate partner told me that perhaps it was time to follow my heart's desire. It was time to follow my bliss. This statement is key to this lesson. I listened and decided to go into medicine and holistic coaching. I was introduced to professional coaching and certified in life coaching, group coaching, and spiritual coaching.

I am now finishing my Bachelor of Science in Nursing and an internship in psychiatric nursing. Nursing has given me many tools to use in coaching and the importance of evidence-based practices related to healing and living life. I now see the world through the lens of Patient-Centered Care, Spiritual Health and Spiritual Assessment, and Family Nursing Assessments.

I use a myriad of tools and certifications to facilitate people healing people, and being healthy, wealthy, and wise. Being able to bring my life experiences, my healing, and my drive to heal by helping others have created the perfect contribution to philanthropy, community health, and private practice.

The key to lifting low self-esteem is simply this: find all the things holding you back from following your bliss and remove them. From there, like a cork rising to the top of the ocean, you will reach the surface naturally. Rapid ascent is what coaching helps me do for other people.

During my life, several lessons became the foundation on which I could move with confidence and become a solid facilitator and steward of life. Let's call my list My Auspicious 13.

Auspicious means conducive to success; favorable; giving of being a sign of future success. Auspicious also means characterized by success; prosperous. Prosperity means many things to many people. To me, it is living my life from a place of love and power, and knowing when my ego and force are taking over. In my coaching, I use an infused process of our coaching wheel to look at many aspects of one's life, and then we take this information and use it to repattern our thoughts and feelings. Repatterning leaves fertile ground for success, peacefulness, wisdom, and love.

The Auspicious 13

1. Breathe deeply.
2. There are times I wanted to give up and couldn't see the forest for the trees, but I asked for help and kept walking through my life.
3. Show up. Stay in the present moment. Contemplate until you understand your relationship to the world.
4. Feel the love of life, and be grateful for the gift of being here now. If you can't feel the love, this is when it is time to ask for help.
5. Find a way to tell your truth.
6. Never assume anything. You will always be partially wrong when you do.
7. Reach for heart and meaning in all you do.
8. Learn how to repattern your words and inner dialog. Your emotions follow your cognitive powers, and your life and actions follow your thoughts and emotions.
9. Ask for help. Remember we all are connected. No one, no matter how young or old, rich or poor, academically or solely life-educated, survives and thrives alone.
10. Take slow walks in silence and notice your world.
11. Don't take anything personally. Know the difference between power and force.
12. Garden and keep connected to nature. Smile.
13. Love yourself. Do what you need to do to stay in love with yourself so you can radiate this back to the world around you.

In conclusion, looking back addressing my Auspicious 13 allowed me to prosper, and implementing these steps developed a beautiful life full of love and abundance. I moved from a frightened young man into an elder with power, and can now recognize force beginning to take over. The following three actions are my challenge for you. Do these as an ultimate labor of love for yourself, particularly if you cannot quite feel the love for yourself yet, for the people, animals, and nature you love around you.

1. Connect yourself with a coach who can help you organize your hidden palate of talent and resources.
2. Work with a mentor who can help you find and eliminate residual habits and thoughts that maintain low self-esteem, who can help you learn the difference between power and force.
3. Practice with a coach to repattern your thoughts and words with cognitive patterning. Find the vibrancy already in you by removing patterns and habits you may no longer need or desire.

What step could you take today that would transform and enlighten the rest of your life?

If you are in a bad mood go for a walk. If you are still in a bad mood go for another walk. - Hippocrates

Meet Matthew J. Moody

Matthew J. Moody owns a holistic life and wellness coaching practice and resides in Santa Fe, New Mexico. He's earned certifications in life, group, spiritual, real estate, and holistic health coaching.

Living.by.Design is a practice that infuses with many other referring professionals, from social service and philanthropies, as well as churches and medical practitioners. Moody's main private client is one of our presidential and philanthropic families. He is passionate about client's breakthroughs out of low self-esteem, anxiety, addictions, and depression. A nationally accredited EMT, Moody is completing his studies in psychiatric nursing. He plans to teach and coach at schools as well as privately. Moody has earned certifications and training in non-profit and for-profit real estate. His process for coaching includes his seven-pointed star process and teaching through cognitive repatterning.

Moody coaches in the realms of hospitality, philanthropy, and abundance optioning. He is the founder and first executive director of Heartbridge Foundation, which was the inspiration for him entering the effective world of professional coaching. "I started a beautiful community-based non-profit and lost my connection with people in the process of becoming an administrator. Life coaching brought me back to help the community I care for and love directly." Please visit mjmoody.com to work directly with Moody.

TEN

Coaching for Success

By P. Michelle Matlock

COACHING FOR SUCCESS: Self Reflection is a tool that can be used to self-motivate by seriously thinking about what drives you to what you want, your gifts, and your passion. In other words, you must want to live a better life. By doing that, you have to ponder on what makes you who you are in terms of the reason you are put here on this earth. You have to identify with your calling. Some people are aware of what they would like to do but have no motivation to take it a step forward. Instead of working towards your dream, you spend your life miserable, confused, and full of ideas. Your gifts and your passion take a back seat while you aimlessly create a mundane life because you are afraid to challenge yourself or go after the things that make you happy. After living a life of boredom, all of a sudden, you want to make a change. It wasn't until I went back to school to obtain my BA in Psychology that I realized I had to make some serious changes in my life. I felt like a hamster on a speeding wheel. I was moving but I was not going anywhere, especially in the direction that I wanted to go. It is then that I began to coach myself.

Before I share my experience with you on how I coached myself, I have to say that Self Reflection is a tool to empower you. It holds you accountable for your own decisions and actions which will cause you to have a sustainable outcome. What you need to know is that Self Reflection does not mean that you compare yourself with others. Bill Gates said, "Don't compare yourself with anyone in this world...if you do so, you are insulting yourself." Self Reflection does not mean that you allow yourself to be disrespected or devalued by others. Self Reflection does not mean that you blame others for your mistakes and wrong doings. Self Reflection does not mean that you are exempted from your responsibilities.

Self Reflection does not mean that in order to shine one has to lower their standards to make others happy. Self Reflection does not mean that you will allow yourself to engage in toxic relationships that would only rob you of your joy, and leave you depressed and full of shame and despair. Self Reflection does not give you permission to find fault in the lives of others while not correcting the faults in your own. Instead, Self Reflection is a process that one can use to empower oneself. Self Reflection allows you to be able to identify any area of your life where there is a need for change in order for adequate growth to take place. It does not matter if there is a professional, financial, health and wellness, spiritual, emotional, or relationship problem. Once you have identified your challenges, and acknowledged your need to make adjustments, the next step is to think back to your past. By pondering the past, you get to reflect critically as you consider those aspects of your past that may have prevented you from advancing towards your goals. In my time, one of the realizations I have come to is that it is important to first, be aware of what it is that makes you happy in terms of what it takes to get you motivated. Secondly, I realized that I had to be specific and intentional in setting goals; and lastly, I became aware that in order to attain my goals, that I must execute a step by step plan, based on my previous realizations.

There are three experiences that I would like to share. One of these has to do with my relationships, with the other two having to do with the struggles that I had encountered with regard to my weight, and how I came to the realization that this journey of my destiny is a process, and not a quick fix or overnight change.

As a young teen, I can recall hearing that all men cheat and they cannot be trusted. When I grew up and was allowed to date, all the things I heard as I was growing up, came back to my remembrance. I started thinking about how unfair it would be was I to fall in love and give my heart to one man, only for him to run out on me with another woman. Before too long, fear had taken root, and a serious case of lack of trust had conquered my being. During the early stage of my life, I had made a conscious decision that I would never get married. Being a person that was honest and outspoken, I found myself trapped in a world of confusion. Although I would tell myself I would never get married, deep down inside, I was fully aware that I wanted to have a husband and children. I immediately got scared.

As time went on, I became more and more bitter, and I knew in that state of mind that I would never be a good wife, let alone a good girlfriend simply because internally, I was a mess. I realized then that I was not ready to be in relationship with anybody until I had done some internal work on myself. This led me to spending more and more time alone as I tried to find myself and do the work that was necessary to bring me the kind of healing that I desired, and that I deserved.

I started praying and crying out to God because I needed help in order for me to become the person that I was created to be. During this period of self-reflection, it was imperative for me to be deliberate and to engage in a thorough process of digging deep into myself.

By coaching myself through Self Reflection, one of the things I had to do was to be true to myself and stand in my truth. I acknowledged that my fears, insecurities, and lack of trust were the leading causes of my inability to enter and maintain a committed relationship; it was then that I started to feel empowered. I came to the conclusion that my destiny and success start with me.

I struggled with my weight. The older I grew, the clearer it became to me that I had to take personal responsibility for my actions. I had poor eating habits that were not easy to change. Eventually, I had to hold myself accountable because I had to be responsible for my own actions.

After I had enrolled back in college to work on my BA, I was not exercising nor was I eating the best of food that was of any nutritional value to the body. I thought that I needed to invest in my health and well-being. I saw an opportunity to do something about my situation, because quite frankly, it was up to me, and only me to do so.

I decided to sign up with Planet Fitness. Exercising made me feel more energized, and cleared my mind from the stresses of life. I felt so good. I started eating healthier. I am living in my truth. I am not perfect; therefore, I embrace who I am.

We all have the tools within ourselves to do whatever it is that we want to do without being apologetic. I used the tools to empower myself, and to embrace the challenge in order to feel good about myself, and to have healthy relationships.

In this relationship, I have grown and was able to fight through the different issues that came and that would have in times past caused me to run from. Being in a relationship allowed me to learn about my mate as well as to learn who I am when I am with him. I never thought that I would come to a place of happiness where I would contemplate marriage. I am on the road to fulfilling one of my life desires.

We all have dreams and desires and are passionate about something or another. Most times our past prevents us from fulfilling our dreams. One thing we all have to remember is everyone we meet has something to teach us and sometimes we have to look back into our past experience so that we can remember and hopefully learn something from it. Pain, frustration, and regret are all a part of the journey to our destiny. This is why I have come away from my experience with a winner's attitude—because I am a conqueror. I can now take my story to the world, letting others know not only that my God has done it again, but that if He could have done it for me, He can do it for them as well!

No one wants to be stuck in a place where there is no growth or change. That is a difficult situation to be in. When there is no one there to P.U.S.H. us through, we have to pray until something happens. We have to tell ourselves that we will have a successful life, whatever our understanding of success is.

Are you in a place of confusion and you do not know what it is that you are supposed to be doing? Do you need someone to coach you, to hold you accountable for your actions, and to help you find your niche to a better life?

Meet Michelle Matlock

P. Michelle Matlock works with individuals that struggle with mental health issues. She helps them in becoming self-sufficient after being integrated into the community from State facili-

ties. They are provided with tools and the resources in order to transition into a more independent consumer as they reside in group homes within our community. While getting them to take responsibility for their own action, it allows them to be more accountable for their own behavior.

She has over twenty years of experience helping teens and adults in identifying their issues and executing a plan in solving their own problems. She also has fifteen years working in a school setting with teens.

She has an Associate Degree in Liberal Arts. She has a Bachelor Degree in Psychology. She was trained in becoming a Certified Professional Life Coach.

When she is not working as a problem solver or in teaching mode, she enjoys traveling with her son, family and friends; she enjoys writing short stories on relationships; enjoys crocheting and making jewelry. If you would love to know more about Michelle, she spends a lot of her time on Social Media, especially Facebook. Do not hesitate to contact Michelle at Sbbpmmat69@yahoo.com or 609-321-1972.

ELEVEN

Anxiety and Panic Attacks Only Made
Me Stronger

By Gerald Ruscingno

Once I was convinced that Anxiety and Panic Attacks could not harm me either physically or emotionally, I was able to make the changes necessary to live a normal life.

TWO OF MY main accomplishments were the following:

1. I went from not driving at all to driving on the most difficult highways without fear, panic, or anxiety.
2. I also was not able to sit in a classroom, but years later I earned in a classroom environment two doctoral degrees —one was a doctorate in chiropractic and the other one was a PhD in health sciences. It did not happen overnight but I went from my life being controlled by anxiety to me controlling the anxiety.

Ironically, from the time I was born until the age of nineteen, my life was very easy and enjoyable. I was born into a very good family. There is nothing I can recall needing or wanting. I enjoyed every day in my younger years. I have a sister two years younger than myself. We have been very close our entire lives. Therefore, when you have everything, who would have thought I would wake up one day in my late teens, to find myself burdened with a life of both anxiety and panic attacks.

I remember the day exactly. I was nineteen, and I drove to school feeling tired. As I arrived at school, I began to feel nervous and anxious. My mouth went dry and the muscles on the sides of my head were tightening. My legs felt weak. One of my friends thought I was having a hypoglycemic attack and she purchased fruit for me to eat. I still felt very uneasy. Since I was still able to drive, I drove home and the anxiety and panic seemed to escalate in severity. From that day on the symptoms were relentless.

After numerous tests that ruled out any physical pathology, the next step was a psychotherapist. Anxiety disorders were on my mother's and father's side of the family. My grandmother and others in my family were also prone to anxiety and panic attacks. I was convinced I had a genetic predisposition for anxiety and panic attacks.

It did not help being a biology major. After completing two years of a pre-med program I had no doubt, this disorder was going to be a struggle. My thoughts controlled my intellect, instead of my mind controlling my body. My thought process should have been this: just because I may have a genetic predisposition, genetic predispositions do not have to become this devastating pathology.

Life became difficult and I had been to every type of therapist and was taking a drug called Elavil. I continued going to school, but I often walked out of class since it was too uncomfortable to remain in class. My only option that granted me some comfortability, while completing my last semester of college, was to take my exams in my professor's office. This opportunity gave me freedom of movement when I was anxious.

As life continued, I saw different therapists. One focused on hypnosis, another biofeedback, and another traditional dialogue between patient and therapist. None of these therapies worked for me. Time was moving quickly and I did not feel or see significant improvement.

A few years after college, I applied for my first position in a micro-biology lab and rented my first apartment a mile away from my home. The anxiety was not much easier, but I forced myself to do this for almost two years. I then applied to Chiropractic school and I had to initially defer my acceptance for one year. I did go to Chiropractic College and the anxiety lessened somewhat with a change in medication, which was a drug called Nardil. There were side effects to the medication and the medication did take away the sharp edge, but the anxiety would escalate at times, sometimes related to the stress of the schooling and sometimes it would come out of the blue.

I did graduate, practiced as a Chiropractor for a short period of time and moved into education, first as a Professor and now as an Administrator. I lived in a state of exhaustion from years of anxiety and panic. I knew my quality of life could be better, so I went from one therapist to another, and was open to every technique that was available to me. I read every book regarding anxiety and panic that I could find. I did get some useful information out of the readings.

Years had gone by and I was not where I wanted to be and I knew there was significant improvement for me to make and I was determined to find the correct therapist for me. I did research different therapies and I found life coaching was very helpful. I coupled this with a therapy called Cognitive Behavioral Therapy and my progress with my coach was slow but steady. Anyone working out of panic, anxiety, or phobias needs a life coach specific to working with anxiety patients and a strong knowledge of Cognitive Behavioral Therapy. As an individual you will decide what issues you want to work on specifically (meaning driving, sitting in a restaurant, etc.)—however, it involves practice, practice, and more practice.

For example, if you are fine driving on side streets, but cannot drive on a highway, how do you want to accomplish this? How one individual may accomplish this goal will probably be different than another individual. Your coach will keep you focused on your goals. At times, you may even ask your coach that you may want to change directions in your treatment plan. As I found with regard to driving, I needed a plan and I needed a professional lifestyle coach trained with individuals who have anxiety and panic. It is fine to change the direction in your treatment plan. We all are required to take an active part in our treatment plan.

Coaching, combined with speaking positively to oneself, as well as different aspects of Cognitive Behavioral Therapy I have found to help me, as well as many others with anxiety and panic. This has helped me to become the strong confident individual I had been before my initial anxiety episode.

I cannot stress the importance of maintaining a positive attitude, even when you struggle to do it. I always employ positive statements to be utilized by the client to enforce an enriched coaching session. If a client in the beginning of their sessions is having a difficult time, it is important for clients to realize, that the more they practice, the better their overall results.

The client will measure improvement by not only what they accomplished, but also the level of anxiety is critical in their self-evaluation. Accomplishment by anxiety prone individuals corre-lates with decreased anxiety levels.

It is important to notice that I am telling my story and simulta-neously integrating an overall view of the role of coaching and how for some individuals, coaching and therapy are utilized together.

Small improvements are a better correlation of success, than large improvements. Small improvements, the client can repeat from today to tomorrow or a week from now. These are true improve-ments. I like to use the term the client has **OWNERSHIP** of the goal and will eventually reach a point where they can accomplish that task with minimum to very little anxiety. The anxiety may leave completely. In my personal experience when I accomplished my goals, I noticed that it is the small improvements which gave me the confidence to move to the next goal.

Since each individual is different and their degree of anxiety or panic is different, coaching is not a one size fits all model. I am certain besides having a genetic predisposition to anxiety and/or panic disorders, some individuals have an extra layer of stress that they need to work with.

In Closing: At nineteen years of age, I had no idea where I was going and I questioned what the future would bring. From hard work, coaching, cognitive therapy, and my faith, I was able to accomplish working my entire adult life, as well as completing two Doctoral degrees. I have always been strong-minded, but now I have the strength and desire to help individuals identify anxiety and panic disorders and seek the help they need through a caring and compassionate coach. I was encouraged by friends and colleagues to tell my story and how I was able to change my life to a level that I never thought possible.

My advantage in coaching individuals with anxiety and panic is simple. I lived it. My situation is not a textbook example. Coaching was a significant part of my treatment plan, and as I said earlier in this chapter, I was treated by coaching and cognitive behavioral therapy, before coaching was considered a treatment plan. Why would I be your ideal coach? In my opinion, individuals who have suffered with anxiety and panic relate best to a coach who has experienced their symptoms and lived their pain. This is not to undermine any other health care provider. In my own treatment plan, I sought out individuals who not only have the scientific knowledge, but also experienced my pain. I can be reached by phone at **917-675-1992**, my e-mail **Docjery@aol.com** as well as my website being **anxietyandpanichelp.com.**

Jerry has practiced as a Chiropractor, and has taught at the University level for over twenty years. He has specialized in teaching Anatomy and Physiology, and Microbiology. Jerry is a life coach for individuals who are afflicted with a combination of anxiety, panic attacks, and phobias. Since he suffered with panic attacks and anxiety and was helped with coaching, determination, and therapy, he became a certified coach.

He had suffered with anxiety and panic for years and through coaching and therapy he has made significant accomplishments as he helped others, but also helped himself. Jerry changed his life from anxiety and panic to one of peace and happiness.

His mission in life is to help others both understand that anxiety and panic attacks cause suffering, but that this is reversible. Jerry's real life story was a difficult one, as he suffered with panic and anxiety. Jerry's coaching experience has helped him achieve balance, happiness. and joy.

Please visit my website anxietyandpanichelp.com.

Please text or call me at 917-675-1992 and my e-mail address is Docjery@aol.com for additional questions or inquires.

For those who read this chapter, please send me your e-mail address and I will keep you on my mailing list. Stay positive.

TWELVE

You Can't See the Label from Inside the Jar

By Nan DeGroat

I FIRST MET my Life Coach Peter Heymann, at a business networking event. I certainly didn't go to this BNI event expecting to hire a Life Coach. I always felt like "life coaching" was a waste of time and especially money! I also believed life coaching was for excuse makers who can't get themselves together.

After speaking for quite some time, he brought up valid points as to why people might want a coach in their life. He equated a life coach to a coach of a sports team. Their purpose brings out hidden potential in the individual players and the potential those individuals have as one unit. Since we incorporate accountability coaching in our weight loss program, the discussion we had about his coaching business and why he loved his resonated with me. Before the luncheon was over, we both agreed it would be fun and beneficial to complete one another's programs.

The intake form I filled out made me think of things I really hadn't given much thought to before, like—what has been my proudest accomplishment? Greatest passion? What was my satisfaction level in different areas of my life like health, career, friends, family…?

And then, "What results are you looking for from coaching?" Results? I wasn't expecting anything at all.

We started with self-discovery exercises challenging me with why I believed people loved me. And then I had to think of all my strong suits—the qualities I developed over the years either out of necessity due to my living conditions or were just a natural strength or quality I have. My strong suits were pretty easy, but the "lovable list," as he called it, was difficult. I didn't know why people liked or loved me.

He told me after only spending a few hours with me he could see many things were lovable about me. I was very surprised when he said compassionate, caring, and genuine. After he explained why he felt the way he did, I agreed with him, but it was difficult for me to think of those good things on my own. I never have a problem telling people about my faults and shortcomings, but I did have difficulty seeing the positive effects I had on others. Having an outsider's perspective greatly affected my self-esteem.

Every week during our session, I realized that the more I spoke the more I processed. The deeper I dug into thought patterns and reactions, the keener my sense of awareness became.

The relationship between Coach Pete and I was an honest one and he made it clear that he was there to support the new me and not allow the old me, which was my negative perspective, to be a bully. He made me aware of how my negative unsupportive thought patterns were just habits—they were not related to my DNA, they were just bad habits that could be changed.

Normally when I would revert to bad habits, I would get frustrated and think, *What's the use?* But, with him speaking to me weekly, I was consistently reminded of my new way of thinking. That outside the jar cheerleader made a difference.

One month of coaching turned into three more. I continued my coaching relationship with him, which allowed me to learn so much about myself. I was a mother of three, part time waitress, and full-time college student who won state awards for excellence in academics. In my eyes, I should have done this when I was eighteen like everyone else did instead of getting pregnant. Really? He called me out on that one, as he should have! He taught me how accomplishments are proof of the ability to change, but again I never saw it from that perspective before. I needed to slow down and take time to enjoy the moment, enjoy my accomplishments, and stop saying "It's no big deal."

Coaching allowed me to discuss the past but only with intentions of understanding it, never to dwell in it. I spoke of past situations briefly and then Peter would direct me into the present saying things like, "What skills did you acquire from that experience?" Or, "How can you separate the facts from the emotions?" And once I did, I could step outside the emotion and look at my circumstance from reality—as an adult who does not need to carry the burden any longer, or as an adult who is no longer living in the past situation. My new mindset helped me stop feeling, thinking, and acting as if I was still a helpless child. Because I opened myself up to new ideas, tools, and practices, I learned how to climb outside of my jar and have a different perspective. My life has not been the same since I developed that super power.

Allowing someone into my life and giving him permission to question my way of thinking and challenging my belief systems was very beneficial. He was able to show me how my reactions or words reflected old beliefs being used as a compass for current adult decisions. It was second nature for me to react or think in a certain direction and I didn't realize I could change it. I didn't realize I could walk away at any time and choose to be different. I could abandon old unsupportive, abusive belief systems at any point! It was so liberating having someone from the outside tell me that I could walk forward without fear!

Our weekly visits became more significant to me than I had imagined. Peter helped me design and prioritize bite size attainable goals. Because of my fear about procrastinating I always wanted to eat the whole pie in one bite, but he would not let me do that. Part of life coaching is helping a person set goals, keep balance, and continue to practice new supportive habits and mindsets. Without this, it's easy to feel ineffective with tasks which don't have a beginning and an end.

When we spoke weekly, I had to tell him what I did or didn't get accomplished. Having him to "answer to" about things was a very big motivator. Having someone help me focus on other goals besides work goals was a big deal. The work I did with him was about me and my personal goals, many of which were realized. Keeping the outside world balanced with my inner needs was very important.

Balance is a very important topic in coaching. It was the one key ingredient I needed help with all the time. I needed to balance work and family, goals and rest, doing too much for others, and not doing enough for me. If I didn't finish everything today, it was ok. My fear of slipping into procrastination was exactly what made me procrastinate, but he was there to remind me of accomplishments and gave me permission to rest and take it all in, but more importantly, understand that resting wasn't procrastinating (which I saw as failure), it was stopping, taking it all in, and enjoying what was done. He kept reminding me that I was a terrific person and how I always strived for personal growth and just needed to practice the new belief systems every day. Mistakes were an opportunity for growth and gentleness toward self; change is a process.

A strong desire to change doesn't ensure its inevitability. It takes practice, determination and a willingness to see your imperfections. I learned to fail forward. I also learned that at first it is DUTY, then it is DESIRE, then it's DELIGHT. It's repeated action and it takes the ability not to get annoyed with yourself when you don't feel like doing it. To reach for help and delegating is essential. Peter gave me permission to ask for help. When someone else told me that it was ok, I stepped into a whole new world of realization. When I don't ask for help, or I don't accept help, I am either missing out on a valuable perspective from an outsider or I'm taking someone else's opportunity to bless me.

If I didn't let someone else into my world, I would not have seen many of the things that held me back. I found someone who was experienced at walking away from old belief systems, breaking old habits, and starting new ones. Therefore, he had the ability to help me do the same thing. He taught me not to rely on the world around me to be my cheerleader. The reality is not everyone will agree or support you. He reminded me to have positive inner dialogue and to always choose edifying thoughts.

Having an outsider illuminate your unique qualities is invaluable. Having someone who is willing to challenge you is equally irreplaceable. And, while you may not be able to see your lovable qualities or strong suits, when other people around you do, listen, take it in, and say thank you!

What do you think your label says?

When people read the ingredients on your jar's label, what do they read?

Take action today. If you are someone who would like mentoring or has been struggling with a weight issue and knows that dieting alone does not help with permanent weight loss, visit my website at breakthroughm2.com and click the "Start Here" link.

Meet Nan DeGroat

Nan DeGroat
Mentor and CEO of Breakthrough M2—Weight Loss & Transformation

Nan DeGroat started her adult life without a plan or a clue. She had three children by age twenty-seven (the first two were born when she was eighteen and twenty). After waitressing for eleven years, she decided to go back to college. She graduated with honors with a Master's degree in education and math. Four years after getting tenure,  she had a major breakthrough with her weight and clarity about her relationship with food. She resigned her teaching position to start her own company—Breakthrough M2 Weight Loss & Transformation.

Now, six years later her business has helped thousands of people lose weight and keep it off. It was this path that led her to being a certified health coach through IIN (Institute of Integrative Nutrition) and receive her board certification as an ND (Naturopathic

Doctor) through Trinity School of Natural Health. Her latest venture was not only going through Wainwright Global and earning a certificate in Professional coaching, but also having her entire staff get certified with her. Her understanding of overcoming a difficult start, living in the real world while trying to grow a family, be a wife, a CEO, and be true to self is what makes her perspective so unique and ability to make connections so valuable to her clients.

THIRTEEN

Honor the Authentic You

By Linda Woodgate

I AM a Global Educator with Personal Transformational Programs, and take a natural approach to Whole Health and everyday living.

I support you in the following ways:

- To be the Authentic You, more and more each and every day
- To feel joy every moment of every day
- To feel supported
- To be encouraged
- To have alternative thought processes in your very own customized "Tool Box," for when the going gets tough
- To celebrate with you small steps to your success
- To be reminded of the positive sides of your journey creating the Success of the Authentic You

Let me support you to create permanent change in your approach to weight, wellbeing, and whole health. Together we can find suitable solutions for your uniqueness, whilst creating a positive and JOY filled approach to YOUR life.

You so deserve this!

My Passion

I love to create space for people to grow and understand their journey more easily and effortlessly. My joy is supporting you to

- discover your true life's purpose and how to get there;
- live the life where you love to laugh at your antics, whilst understanding the stories that the mind creates;
- feel in charge of who you are and where they are and feeling good about that;
- feel the smile go all the way down your body because you have the tools to be happy;
- love all the unique moods you can come up with and know you have the choice to change them and feel proud of making that happen.

My aim in working with you is to

- clearly understand your vision, needs, and objectives;
- help you to develop the plans to move quickly and easily toward your goals;
- provide support to ensure you are nurtured and motivated to achieve your vision;
- celebrate your victories with you.

Successful Coaching is about

- asking you the right questions;
- supporting you to decide for yourself, what your goals are and how you can achieve them;
- listening, understanding, and helping you to prioritize your goals;
- enabling you to clearly articulate your desires;
- helping you to stay on track with your objectives.

I look forward to helping you to

- clearly identify and articulate your goals and desires;
- develop strategies to overcome setbacks;
- identify and eliminate limiting beliefs;
- be accountable to your vision;
- step outside of your comfort zones to achieve your goals.

What Is an Everyday Living Coach?

I feel that for people to change and appreciate themselves they need short and easy ways to achieve that, every day, with small steps of awareness in everything they do.

I give people things to feel, think about, talk about, but most of all to be able to smile, laugh, or giggle about. These are the "tools" I put in people's "tool boxes" so they can use them any time, any place, anywhere, whatever they are doing or feeling.

As an Everyday Living Coach, I focus on how to **respond in the present**, rather than react from the past, or complicate the future.

What Makes You Whole and Healthy?

To recognize that there are four very important parts of you that make up the team of your uniqueness:

- The Physical, Emotional, Mental, and Spiritual (Spiritual being your belief systems)
- All these parts need to work together as a team to create the energized, positive, and loving of you, and yourself
- Your unique "Tool Box" that can be influenced to enable you to respond in the present

Tools for Your Tool Box

I would love to share some ideas to work towards giving you valuable tools for your Tool Box.

To create small steps of change:

- It doesn't just apply to work or to home.
- It applies to all of your life including the mind chatter.
- It doesn't have to be a chore.
- It doesn't have to be a "thing" that you "have" to make time for.
- It doesn't have to be arduous.
- It can be fun. It has to make you smile, laugh, or giggle.
- It has to help you see the sunshine in every moment of the day.

Some practical exercises you can implement when doing everyday activities include:

- Move your weight from one foot to the other.
- Hold your tummy in to the count of three and release and keep on going.
- Smile and laugh lots.
- Focus on your breathing and recognize what it is doing.
- Check you are breathing evenly, and expand each breath a little each time.

These ideas apply to any thing you feel is a "chore" or difficult to do. Think of a way to make it feel better for you. Think of ways to distract your mind from seeing it as negative. If you apply some happy ideas to everything you do, life will begin to change.

For example:

Think about having to do the dishes after a meal—is this a chore? This is a metaphor for a clean start and renewed beginnings!

- Sing your favorite song as you do the dishes. Focus on how wonderfully clean the dishes look and you feel proud to serve delicious food on them.
- Listen to your favorite singer/program that brings a smile to your face.
- Throw your emotions in the dirty dishwater and let them flow away and fill that space with a gorgeous picture of your favorite flower

How to Prepare for Physical Challenges and Changes

It is good to honor your body as your creation even though there may be "bits" you don't like.

If we don't like us, how can anyone else love us?

Our physical being is the carrier and keeper of all that we are, so taking care of it is essential. We all have different ideas of what that means and how that needs to happen for us.

Here are few things to start you in the direction of feeling good for YOU:

- When you walk anywhere, walk from the hips and hold your tummy in.

- Focus on your body and your breathing and not any distractions like headphones or mobiles.
- What is your body doing? Aching? Are your strides even?
- If something aches when you are at your desk or out walking, focus and change your position.

How to Prepare for Emotional Challenges and Changes

Understand that emotions belong to you and honor that you put them there to take care of you at some stage in your life. Maybe it was last year or many years ago when you were two or ten years old. They don't really serve you well now—you have grown in so many ways since!

My suggestions and reflections to control these experiences include

- take a breath;
- think before you speak;
- check if you are speaking from the Reaction of your "filing system" or can you BE in the Present moment and Respond;
- Anger versus Anger creates Fireworks; Anger versus Calmness has nowhere to go but defuse.

How to Prepare for Mental Challenges and Changes

When in a situation you have a choice to *react* or *respond*.

If you feel yourself reacting with defense mechanisms you are coming from your "Filing System" (the subconscious mind) which has stored everything you have ever done. This is filed by all your senses. Senses of smelling, touching, seeing, hearing, and tasting.

With the everyday "tools" I teach you and finding some for yourself, life can be and will be more positive, more alive, more fun, more manageable for you.

In order to respond with a clear mind and in the moment:

- Take a breath. Listen and focus on the whole conversation until the end. Ask yourself are you waiting to answer before that person has finished?
- Be prepared to acknowledge their point of view and offer rather than tell yours as an alternative.

How to Prepare for Spiritual Challenges and Changes

When I talk about spiritual I mean your belief system which was created at an early age.

Understanding and accepting that this is your unique perspective on life, allows you to be more tolerant about other people's belief systems.

The next time you are in conversations about "right or wrong" or "good or bad," learn to be curious:

- Ask questions from a curious rather than a defensive view.
- Listen carefully without applying your control beliefs.
- You are allowed to agree to disagree but only when you have listened carefully to the full story.
- Constructive discussion leads to more harmony of acceptance of human differences.

Summary

I am obsessive about supporting you to make life more fun and positive with ease and grace; to be able to give you ways of making life less complicated and more enjoyable is my passion and goal. I love to share my amazing life experiences and help you laugh, and love you, and BE you. I am constantly overwhelmed with joy and unconditional love for you and the changes you allow yourself to make on your amazing journey of life.

So some quick points in summary for you to take away with you:

- Think before you speak.
- You have choices. You can change if you want to.
- Don't ask the people around you to change to suit you.
- You change to be the Authentic You, whatever that may be. That does not include negative words, feelings or outbursts. They just don't help you or the people around you; it just creates tension, unhappiness, anger, and upset —why would you want to do that?
- Why do you need to get your own way?
- Is your way the right way? Maybe for you but not for everyone.
- Is the situation you find yourself in life threatening? No? Then smile and walk away. You will feel so much better and in control of your only mind and your only body.
- You are AMAZING and remember that, each and every day.

Meet Linda Woodgate

A wealth of life experiences in corporate, media, and the forces have shaped me into a gifted communicator with the ability to share and teach others in a relaxed and approachable way.

As an experienced Life Coach, Laughter Yoga Leader, Workshop Facilitator, Spiritual Teacher, Indian Head Massage practitioner, and several other modalities, I have observed the level of stress prevalent in clients and audiences. By meshing components of

several modalities I have responded to this with a program specifically aimed at reducing stress and "moving moods" in very simple, practical, and fun ways.

I support my clients to find clarity, confidence, creativity, and excitement in their lives, and enable them to share their story with passion to anyone, anytime, anywhere. I am passionate about helping others to realize the changes they seek and to make it happen with ease and relative speed. I am able to offer very comprehensive information and tools that you can easily integrate in your daily life to support your emotional, mental, spiritual, and physical well-being.

My deep and compassionate understanding of others is reflected in my favorite mantra, "Live, Laugh, and Love Your Moments!"

Contact Linda Woodgate

- lindawoodgate@live.com
- +64 21 188 5778
- Skype: Linda Woodgate
- lindawoodgate.com
- facebook.com/SuccessOfTheAuthenticYou

FOURTEEN

Empowered Relationships through Powerful Listening

By Rev. Robert Turner, DMin, BCC

EFFECTIVE COMMUNICATION IS SPEAKING POWERFULLY and persuasively. In relationships, the core of a couple's bond is the ability to actively listen. Powerful listening can facilitate a shift to positive communication, opening new possibilities in a relationship.

The Speaker

To empower a partner to listen effectively, the speaker must communicate to not only be heard, but understood. Take responsibility for effective conversations with your partner.

The Listener

Your partner's ability to listen is affected by "noise"—distractions, loud sounds, or even emotional bias. Emotional noise includes past events that will impact your partner's understanding of your words. Become more effective in your communication by recognizing *how* your partner hears you. Break through the noise, and you will begin to speak in a way that is most impactful to your listener.

Nine Listening Styles

Without awareness of the way you listen, you are at the mercy of your own style—you will "hear" only what fits the patterns for which you are listening. There are nine common listening styles that may impact your ability to empower your relationship.

1. Looking Good

It's impossible to hear someone else when your attention is on yourself. Partners obsessed with looking good are too busy composing what they will say next, rather than listening to what is actually being said. As a result, you overlook what is important to the other person, since you value "how you appear" over a direct conversation.

How to overcome:

- Shift your focus from your next response to your partner's actual words, in real time.
- Take that moment to honor your partner.
- Shift focus from yourself to support your partner's needs.
- If your partner is always trying to "look good," use silence. Silence will quiet your partner's thought process, engaging him or her to really listen to what you are saying.

2. Taking Things Personally

Have you ever thought that your partner did something just to irritate you? Many times your partner's concerns have absolutely nothing to do with you. This listening style may make you feel rejected or insulted when your partner is addressing his or her needs, concerns, or commitments.

How to overcome:

- Be willing to listen to what your partner is actually saying, rather than what you believe you are hearing.
- Realize that what your partner is saying is about him or her—not about you.
- If your partner has this listening style, gently address your partner's reaction, showing him or her that your comments are related to something other than him or her.

3. Validation

This listening style is often accompanied by its twin, "looking good." Validators are continuously looking for confirmation of your love in the words you speak. Listening for validation can severely hamper empowering communication between a couple.

How to overcome:

- Guard against interpreting what your partner means by listening to what your partner is actually saying.
- Take the attention off yourself.
- If you find yourself invalidated, remember that no one can diminish your self-esteem without your permission.
- In the moment you feel invalidated, express your feelings to your partner. This allows your partner to clarify the situation.
- If your partner exhibits this listening style, reiterate your thoughts in a clear way.

4. Being Offended

Partners with this listening propensity appear to be always "looking for trouble." The offended don't seem happy until they find something to complain about.

How to overcome:

- Look for words that empower, rather than offend you.
- Distinguish between what was actually said and how you interpreted it.
- Learn to distinguish the difference between the sound of the other person's voice and the noise inside your own mind.
- Identify which elements are your responsibility, and generate different, less negative interpretations which empower your relationship.
- If your partner says something that you interpret as offensive, shift your interpretation to one that supports you.
- If your partner exhibits this listening style, ask them to explain his or her feelings. Overcome his or her objections with factual feedback to reiterate your intended meaning.

5. I Already Know

This listening style is most common among couples who have been together for a long time. Your familiarity with how your partner communicates and responds to situations sometimes leads to assuming rather than listening.

How to overcome:

- Understand the power of staying open to the possibility that you could have misread the situation or your partner's intentions.

- Recognize new ways to explore what you don't know.
- Give yourself permission to not know, and then listen to your partner for new possibilities. Your breakthroughs will come as a result of your willingness to "try on" a new idea or concept, one of which you were not previously aware.
- If your partner possesses this listening style, ask them to be willing to set aside past assumptions in order to look objectively and explore any new possibilities.
- Remind yourself and your partner about your shared commitment to be open to new ideas and ways of thinking.

6. Quick Closure: Get to the Answer, Fast!

Communication is not a drive-through window. Empowered relationships take time and a willingness to speak, share, and listen. A partner who listens for quick closure is not willing to make the time to explore other angles and possibilities. So much is missed when a conversation comes to a quick, premature end. Information is not always shared in a clear concise way, especially between two people who are in a long relationship.

How to overcome:

- Slow down. Be deliberate in your speech, patient in your listening, and measured in your response.
- Manage your need to know the answer right away.
- Be open to less visible possibilities.
- If your partner has this listening style, be clear. Avoid using tedious details and focus instead on concise concepts.

7. Resignation

Listening with resignation is often linked to a past relationship failure. For example, a partner who experienced a past episode of infidelity may believe that such behavior is inevitable. As such, he or she overreacts whenever the mere prospect of a repeated instance may surface, no matter how remote.

Resignation can decimate a couple's enthusiasm. It causes relationships to lose hope and negative expectations to become self-fulfilling prophecies.

New relationships are generally open to new possibilities. As years pass, the sea of resignation rises to drown them in the negative. Partners who listen with resignation are comfortable with the reasons things can't be done and shouldn't even be attempted.

How to overcome:

- Train yourself to generate conversations that lead to possibilities, which will generate relationship vitality and a happy and successful rapport.
- Seek discussions about possibilities: your dreams, inspirations, and aspirations. This may seem awkward at first, especially if your relationship has experienced significant challenges in the past. Inspire hope in your partner, and the attitude that anything is possible with love, partnership, commitment, and determination.
- If your partner exhibits this style, ask for clarification on the basis of his or her feelings. Remind him or her about your current status, and how things are now different from his or her past.

8. Judging

In today's culture of judgement, this listening style takes drawing conclusions to an art form. There's nothing new, nothing to be learned. Such a listening style stifles any new possibilities for you and your partner to grow together.

How to overcome:

- Recognize when you are listening in a way that inhibits your relationship.
- Determine if judgmental listening supports what you really want from your relationship.
- Generate a more powerful listening attitude to better support your relationship.
- If your partner exhibits this listening style, create an opening for them to be willing to try something new. Ask your partner to be willing to put aside that which is already "known" to evaluate it with a fresh, open mind.

9. Brevity

Perhaps you're tired of reading this list. If so, perhaps you have this listening style. This is also the cousin of style six, "quick closure." Impatient listeners often want the other person to get to the point quickly, without any superfluous content. This is even more difficult if the partners have differing listening styles—before a laid-back partner finishes his or her story, the "hurry up and get to the point" partner is off somewhere else, having dismissed the conversation as worthless due to its slow pace.

How to overcome:

- If you find yourself listening impatiently, try to stay present and engaged.
- Be patient and understanding. Use body language to encourage progress, without being dismissive.
- If your partner exhibits this listening style, ask them

follow-up questions to engage them during the conversation. This will make the discussion more interactive—and allow for your partner to understand your need for more detail.

Exercises for Powerful Listening

Consider these exercises to establish your listening style, and how it affects your relationship:

- Engage in a dialogue with your partner to determine your most prevalent listening style, and how each of your styles contribute to, or detract from, your relationship.
- Keep a daily journal that tracks the way you listen. Note how your listening style changes, especially during stressful interactions. Review your journal together weekly, and work together to see how you can change your behavior.

Conclusion

Hey, are you still listening? See, you're already making progress. As you review this listing, you may have discovered that you employ more than one of these styles at any given time. When you identify how you listen, you will be able to change your behavior. As a result, you will become a better, more powerful listener—resulting in a stronger, more empowered relationship.

Rev. Dr. Robert Turner is a senior pastor with over thirty-five years of professional experience, board-certified life coach and certified relationship coach who specializes in helping individuals and couples turn their relationships around and become the best couple they can be. Stagnant relationships can turn into strong, successful marriages with Dr. Turner's services, which include

premarital coaching, wedding consultation and officiating, marriage coaching, and professional speaking. He has been happily married for over nineteen years, officiated more than 700 weddings, and led thousands of coaching sessions.

For more information

- Visit: RelationshipCoachTurner.com
- Contact: Robert@RelationshipCoachTurner.com

FIFTEEN

I Am a Fighter By Nature

By Shari Salomon

WELCOME TO MY WORLD. I am a Health/Wellness Nutrition Coach, a fitness instructor, personal trainer, Recovery Coach, gym owner, Reiki Master, mother of three college age girls, wife…I can keep going of course…we all know how this goes. I'm a daughter, sister, and a lifeline to friends and clients. I wear an awful lot of hats. I am what you would call a "middle aged" woman. So why do I take on writing a chapter in a book when busy is an understatement in my life? I took on this project with the hope, if nothing else, of saving just one person. With Coaching I have found my calling, my purpose, to heal others. I feel if you come away from my writing with the thought, *Wow, she has been there, she understands,* then I have accomplished what I'm striving for here. I work hard every day on myself. I take care of my body for me, work, and my health. I get my workouts in. I even go as far as to schedule "Me Time" into my calendar. It's actually scheduled at 4 a.m.! I get up for me. I'm the important part of this story. My meditation sessions are for me. I eat clean, stay fit, I'm a fighter by nature. I fight a disease called PMDD—Premenstrual Dysphoric Depression. With all I have in me, I strive to make it through everyday. It's a challenge I didn't offer to take on, didn't want, but it was thrust upon me. I now learn more with each episode that I go through.

Someone recently said, I'm closer to grandparenthood, than having another baby myself. This is definitely true, just in no rush to get there. Right now I am happy admitting middle aged, thinking this doesn't seem so bad. I have been told I look younger than I actually am. I have chosen clean eating as my wellness option. It's what serves my body best, the way I'm used to living. I try hard to instill certain mantras into my day. Always suggesting to people, "That every day is a new adventure, enjoy the journey." This is an optimistic way of seeing the rollercoaster ride of emotions I live. Now I really try hard to embrace "Live What You Love." I love helping people to see their goals and aspirations within their own grasp. I admit and believe I'm past that middle number. I accept each day as it comes. I expect that I will use today to grow and every day I'm given to better my world around me, mentally, physically, and emotionally.

My world is a tight circle. It is one that allows few inside my deep, sometimes very dark, emotions. Emotions that are sometimes under the influence of my PMDD. I keep a tighter hold on my own goals and aspirations. I find it a little easier to share the raw, vulnerable side of the disease I fight. When you are able to see, hear, and feel the challenges in front of you, you can become more open to the roadblocks and challenges that are getting in your way.

As a coach I work to validate these roadblocks, help you to see that these are very real situations, even difficult to get through. Some try to solve roadblocks by pretending they don't exist, completely ignoring them, going over them, or even attempting to dig a hole to go under them. Yes, that's the same as hiding. Roadblocks are there to challenge us. They allow us to get down to the raw, unexposed part of ourselves. I help people by reminding them that these are only roadblocks, a speed bump at the moment. Although it feels like you are trying to fight, with all you have against the world. We work together to guide you. Using different methods, as well as asking questions you couldn't ask yourself. Then together we try to instill that you remember the good in yourself so you can allow yourself to feel that getting through the roadblock is not completely out of the question, like you thought before we met.

My clients and I find each other in many ways. Sometimes on a treadmill, sitting in a local restaurant having a drink, or even on vacation. I'm a believer in "There is a reason we met today." The reason we came upon each other, the reason, even if you are not open to it yet, will find a way into your life. One day you will come back to me to let me know you got through your roadblock. That is what I mean about meeting for a reason. Just that I give people a new perspective. They can see through another set of eyes, ears, and discretion.

Recently I started to embrace the newer mantra, without eliminating the old, "Every day is a new adventure, enjoy the journey." I just found it harder to believe in only this, due to my mental health situation. My newly adapted "Live What You Love" makes more sense to my brain at this moment. Live what you love, why wouldn't we try this? Believing that we can embrace both. Happiness is an amazing proponent of optimal health. If you are living what you love you will soar each day. Meet new heights and fulfillments, new goals or adventures, a throwback to the older mantra, every day being a new opportunity to get it right, achieving new and better. If you enjoy what you do every day, how you feel doing it, you will want to embrace both ways of thinking with me. You can love the everyday adventure and live for it.

As my recovery coaching mind begins its journey, a whole new set of questions occurs. Have you ever put words to paper that you wish never existed? Maybe you never wanted anyone else to know you had actually taken the time to write them. For sure you never thought you would want to share these words with others. I have written something, I wish I never had a chance to write. Although, at the time of the writing, it felt necessary and appropriate. I do wish this letter did not exist. It can't be unwritten, so instead I chose to share my story. I have that letter locked away in my computer. It was for noone to ever see, hopefully never need to see or find. It is a letter of feelings I wish I hadn't had, a bad day in the life of, so to speak, which brings us back to the first mantra. Some days are harder to enjoy than others. More than that, I wish that those words were never worthy of being written. They are words worth putting behind me, so I can embrace living what I love. I truthfully don't want anyone to see that letter, but more because when I think of it, I start to feel what I have written was selfish in some way. It is a suicide letter, saying goodbye, wishing love and happiness to the ones who loved me that I would be leaving behind. They would be going on without me. As cryptic as I may be about this disease, I strive to make it through every day. I hope that the thoughts that go through my head, will never be something that you experience even once in your lifetime.

With each month, comes new strategies my doctors come up with to keep PMDD where it belongs...far from my thoughts, helping to balance my brain. If only it consistently stayed away! I have looked in the mirror and thought, *What if I end it right here, now?* I've looked at pill bottles, it could be as easy as taking these. One handful or just a few to quiet my brain, for at least the moment. Then I think of my husband, my girls, my parents, siblings, and friends and think one step further and they are what bring me back. I admit thinking of walking into the ocean and never coming out. Just walking out to the horizon where maybe I would find peace for my brain. Luckily that particular time, when I was having that feeling of raw pain from my heart to my head, I caught a glimpse of my then teenage daughter. I was immediately brought back to the here and now. I felt the need to be here. I was not done with this journey yet, which again brings me to "Every day is a new adventure, enjoy each day you get." Living what you love is a blessing. While I fight my PMDD daily, monthly, and yearly, I rely on my coaching skills, as well as the medication prescribed by my doctors. I became a coach to help others, ones who suffer illness, ones who just need to rely on someone else to help pick up the pieces in their worlds. I want wellness for myself as well as for all who come in contact with me. Even in spite of how sometimes we all sabotage ourselves.

Is there is a time in your life, let's say "a day in the life of" you really wish you could undo? But as we know, days like this help us to grow and change. I look forward fulfilling Living What I LOVE. For me it's my family, workouts, and work that help my brain. They keep me busy getting through my day. Listening to the music I love when I work out helps. It's a key part of my wellness. Everyone will have a different release for their brain. Coaching has taught me how to find my release. I hope that sharing my story I have helped you to seek out what you may need. I rely on myself to live each day to its fullest and embrace my mantras. So, please join me and live what you love?

Meet Shari Salomon

Shari Salomon is the owner of 121 for Life. She is a Health/Wellness and Nutrition CPC, as well as a Certified Recovery Coach. As an avid gym lover since her teens, she has become a certified

Personal Trainer, Spinning, Aqua, Core/Balance, Yoga, Reiki Master, and Meditation Instructor. Shari was one of the very early users of "Virtual" training, using a webcam to train clients.

She aspires to help all who come into her path for whatever their purpose. Shari is a firm believer that we all meet for a reason, and is constantly looking to find the answers as to "Why?"

Shari has been married to Michael for twenty-four years and she looks forward to spending many more years together with him as he has been the love of her life since becoming childhood sweethearts at the ages of fourteen and sixteen. Together they have three beautiful and unique adult daughters, Sydney, Molli, and Mackenzie. With their love and support, 121 for Life was created and has begun to successfully thrive. Shari is forever grateful for her wonderful family and an amazing support system. To learn more, visit Shari's website at 121forlife.com.

SIXTEEN

Ho`oponopono

THE MEANING OF LIFE: HOW TO; KNOW IT, FIND IT, LIVE IT.

By Percell Rivere St. Thomass

Until we learn to seek within ourselves that which we cannot see, we relentlessly pursue life with our eyes wide shut.

FOR MOST OF MY LIFE, things simply fell into place. I was able to achieve various degrees of successes without much effort. Yet, I was always seeking something more; not of material or superficial value, but of an inner peace and happiness that seemed forever absent from my achievements and recognitions. Then, one day, "I Re-member-ed."

I have had long and successful careers as a professional actor and dancer, public speaker, teacher, administrator, director, and coach. Though well liked and accomplished, I seemed to always fall short of the types of successes that I thought I should have. Something was lacking, and not allowing me to live my grandest desires.

Even as a child, I had "inherently known" that there is more to life than our daily encounters. I have always "known" that there is another part of life that is...witnessed, but not seen; felt, but not touched. And, I have always "known" that if we cannot learn to manifest "that" part of life... nothing we might gain in "this" part could ever make us truly whole.

As early as age five, I knew the Laws of Attraction, Love, Forgiveness, and Gratitude. Of course, I had no idea of the importance or magnitude of these things, or how to manifest them in my life, and over time, lost much of the insights. As many of you, I grew into adulthood with a nonchalance about the Laws. I passed them off as being: religious batterings of churches long dead, metaphysical or notional jabberwocky of the anti-religious, or, simply the wild control tactics of bullies spouting "holier than thou" agendas without having to do something to prove them. Though, as I continued to move up the ladder of life and never reaching my nirvana, I somehow found the fortitude to not balance on the rung of self-pities, but to want to know why...Why was I not happy?

I wasn't happy with who I was or whom I had become. I wasn't happy with how I looked to myself, or how I was perceived by society. I wasn't happy with where I was: physically, financially, emotionally, or spiritually. I was lost, yet, I was not alone. There was something within me that was familiar, yet fleeting, tangible; yet not which was constantly challenging me. What was this part of me that I could feel but not find?

I began to study myself. This type of study came easily as it was not new; I had been studying, with an air of superior disgust, human behavior and its absurdities for most of life. It became apparent through these journeys inward, that the reason(s) why I was never happy was/were because I had always been operating with and for only a small part of who I was; that there was more to me than, literally, met the eye.

I discovered that we are trinal beings. I came to know our three parts as (1) the physical part that eats, sleeps, and bleeds; (2) the soulful part that is the life which resides within the physical part, and leaves at physical death; and (3) the mind, that part of us which is neither body nor breath, but obviously alive. It was this third one which immediately caught my attention. The thought, no pun intended, of something being able to think, rule, govern, make decisions about my life, be forever hidden from view or touch, but be alive within me was most intriguing. Yet, it also seemed so self-evident that I couldn't not cower in corners occasionally at the embarrassment of my stupidity. How could I have not known this?

The mind is an interesting part of our makeup. I can't say, "...an interesting part of our bodies..." because it isn't a part of our bodies. We cannot see it or touch it. It is not a physical part of us. Yet, it is alive and animate. We know that it exists...but where, exactly? We must redefine it in order to understand it.

We know that the mind also consists of three parts: a subconscious, conscious, and superconscious. So, we begin at the basics.

What is a Subconscious Mind? Simply, it is the worker bee of the mind. It does not work alone. It is a part of the mind which simply follows orders from another part, doing whatever it is told, without question, reason, or hesitation. The subconscious has no thought power, it follows didactic order to the letter. It "mindlessly" does not think or reason. It is perfect for sub-continuous bodily functions such as: breathing, heartbeat, skin rejuvenation, etc. The subconscious gets its orders from the conscious and superconscious mind. By better understanding the subconscious, and how and why it works, we are better able to feed it properly... to give it better instructions to follow. It, in turn, will create better circumstances and possibilities for us, and help us to create better decisions and actions in our every moments.

The Conscious Mind is the guardian of our lives. It controls our thoughts, words, and deeds. From birth, it has learned of all of the things that make up, regulate, and sustain life on the physical plane. It is an amazing curio because it can reason (think), process (work, work out, work through), cogitate (analyze), and contemplate (plan) many things at once. It can learn, change, retain, and forget. The conscious mind can even override the subconscious mind.

It is in the conscious mind, that we spend most of our time. This is most unfortunate, not because we do it—we should—but because of the way in which we use our conscious minds. Unfortunately, practically from birth, we have learned to use the conscious as a sifter for what not to do or have in life. From the first "No," we have processed: what not to say/do, how not to be/act, what rules/laws not to break, etc. It would be far better to use the conscious mind to make choices for all of the things which are positives…that we should do.

Sadly, it seems almost inherent of human behavior that, often, in times of mental or emotional stress, the conscious mind shuts down, and leaves us to the animalistic behavior of the subconscious, a mind with no thoughts or reasons. Therefore, we must be incessantly sentient of what we "consciously" put into it.

The Superconscious Mind is, indeed, our super hero. It is that part of the mind that controls the all of life; that which "we" are, and that which breathes life into all living things. It is literally our connection to Life. We might call it Divine Mind, God, Supreme Being, Universal Consciousness, Creator, or Life Force. It is this super-consciousness that allows us to be human [physical] beings, but born in the "image" of the Creator. We must know that this is not religious hyperbole; it is spiritual fact. The Superconscious also has complete control over our emotions. This, for example, often causes great conflict between a desired physical "feeling" and innate emotions.

The Superconscious is purely non-physical, and lives in the invisible Realm of the Absolute. It gives Life, guarantees Life, and carries out every demand of Life. It is important that we understand this powerful life force, for…

it will create our very lives exactly as we ask of it.

It is important that we understand fully what we want from life, and why, because the Universe can and will create exactly the lives our hearts desire. If we know how to live in the superconscious, it will manifest our dreams, grant us the things that we wish to achieve, make us who we wish to be, and, give us the lives that we wish to live.

It is, indeed, the most important part of the triune mind.

"I have a good mind to…"—"I changed my mind"—these expressions have become so cliché that we take the mind for granted. Yet, it is neither head nor brain, but the intangible part of us that connects us to the all of everything by natural law. Attraction is not that cutesy little thing we sing about in song or read in Hallmark cards. It more so is a force that mutually draws entities together and opposes their separation. The Law of Attraction is a powerful natural state that is inherent in all of us, if we can find it.

The Law of Gratitude is the stepping stone to understanding the Meaning of Life. We must know that all of this has been given to us through natural grace, and to be thankful does not mean to be happy of the receipt, it is to be emotionally gratified or satisfied with the receipt.

To know the Law of Forgiveness is to know the Meaning of Life. This does not mean to forget wrongdoings, but to absolve from your life everything which is not from Love…to erase from obligation or consequence all such thought.

I have come to know that these three graces, but made manifest, are only the beginnings. These Laws and how to live them are the most important lessons in life. I haven't always practiced what I preach. One day, I reunited the three minds; I was re-"mind"-ed of who I am…who we all are. In Hawai`i, we call this Ho`oponopono; living our grandest desires through the basic life principles of True Love.

Today, with a well-earned degree and a better earned knowledge and vigor, based on a lifetime of born wisdom and experiences, both of silver spoons and hard knocks, on and off the path, I live… talk, teach, and coach the Laws of Life. It is my given, driven, and continued purpose and happiness to bring as many as I may to this knowledge.

Meet Percell Rivere St. Thomass

"One of the greatest voices and teachers of my time." – S. Hulderson, Davenport, Iowa

"A profoundly spiritual, yet non-religious, insight into the meaning of life and how to live it; how to understand who by what we are, and, live our greatest potentials." – K. Grooms, Hattiesburg, Mississippi

Teaching the Laws of Attraction, Love, and Forgiveness has been my desire and calling since a young child. By studying such ideologies including: Jesus the Christ, Florence Scovel Shinn, "A Course in Miracles©," Buddha, Mahatma Ghandi, the Dalai Lama, Hawai`ian Ho'oponopono, and more, it has been my profound pleasure—my given, driven, and continued purpose and happiness, to share these fundamental life principles with others, and to help guide them to more fulfilling lives.

FREE CONSULT:

- percellstthomass.com/personal-coaching
- Phone: 601-329-5808
- percellstthomass.com

SEVENTEEN

The Perception Conundrum

By Kathleen Carr

WHAT IN THE world is perception? Do I have it? How does it impact my life? Yes, we all have perception and knowing what it is and how it impacts our lives is a journey everyone can benefit from embarking on. Henry David Thoreau tells us, "We find only the world we look for." Is perception real or imagined? It is both. It is real because neuroscience informs us that information that is perceived is ultimately imprinted in the neurons of our brains. It is imagined because our minds create the *perceptive movie*, then consciously, unconsciously, and sometimes emotionally hold on to it like a security blanket until some change occurs. Why is it important? As humans, we are driven to understand to feel balance and safety in our world. Can I influence my perceptions? Absolutely! First, take a step forward with me to view what perception looks like.

Anatomy of Perception—Natural vs. Acquired

From the moment we are born we are perceiving and communicating. It is in our DNA. Infants are calmed when wrapped tightly in a warm blanket. Babies who are breast fed, instinctively *root* toward the mother's breast. Touch, sound, sight, and nurturing are our first teachers. We innately observe, perceive, and communicate. We continue to gather intelligence throughout our lives which is stored in our subconscious, and is constantly changing and developing. There are many *streams* that feed the development of perception such as our senses, our central nervous system, our environment, our experiences, and our stored subconscious data. Dr. H. Sebastian Seung, Neuroscientist, theorizes regarding the retina of our eyes, "The first steps of perception are actually happening even before the information reaches the brain." Once in the brain, neuro pathways are imprinted with the unanalyzed information. All our experiences and emotional reactions are stored in the subconscious which feeds our perceptions. Our perceptions become our *truth.*

A Google search of the meaning of perception sheds some interesting light for us: *"a way of regarding, understanding, or interpreting something; a mental impression; the state of being or process of becoming aware of something through the senses."* Perception, therefore, denotes an action. Perception, as we mature, is also a complex *stew* of memories, fears, trauma, values, experiences, and environment all mixed together. We draw on it immediately when familiar or unfamiliar circumstances arise.

We are all consciously and unconsciously utilizing our *perceptive filter* multiple times throughout the day to interpret our world, frequently without intention. In our human experience we regularly perceive, communicate, and choose to act on our perceptions, wisely or unwisely, which creates either positive or detrimental impact in our lives. Perception is also a powerful tool for those individuals in positions of authority or leadership who can use it to influence others.

As a group, people are also susceptible to fall into *perceptual camps,* when we are presented with challenges on a large or global scale. This can apply to war, race, immigration, religion, politics, scandals, gender issues, human rights, etc. One example of *perceptual camps,* which was highlighted in the Oscar nominated movie *Spotlight,* is the perception of various groups of people in reaction to the years long evidence of the sexual victimization of children by priests of the Catholic church. Catholic priests in various regions exhibited a pattern of preying on children who were from low income, single parent homes. The church *dealt* with it by covering it up and moving priests to assignments in other geographical locations, often to work with children again. As news became public, people self-divided into *perceptual camps* in response to the news of the abuse. One *perceptual camp,* when made aware of the abuse, exhibited *complete denial,* including many parents. In their perception, such charges were impossible and they accused the exposers of deceit. Their closely held perception that the priests were divine agents of God, and so far as the Catholic institution was concerned, above the law, prevented them from perceiving the copious amount of evidence available. A second *perceptual camp* was suspicious, but conscious that the evidence coming forth might be true. They held limiting perceptions about the personal and institutional consequences they might face should they speak out for justice. Their fear became a barrier to action. Rather than *rocking the boat* they chose silence and indifference. A third *perceptual camp* held perceptions with a high value of justice above all. The perception held by this group is that abuse is unacceptable and it must be addressed. It was this *perceptual camp,* victims, parents, teachers, public officials, and the legal system combined, that shed light publicly and ultimately brought many priests and the church to justice. Of interesting note, the first and second *perceptual camps* actively put pressure on the pro-active people in the third *perceptual camp* to discredit, pay off, undermine, and threaten the group into silence. Uncomfortable? Don't be. Take another step with me to honor your ability to perceive and its many possibilities.

Power of Perception—An Open Door

Our perception is an extremely powerful mind tool that influences our communication, judgement, and choices. However, our perception is also strongly influenced by our emotional state, past experiences, disinformation, stress, and for some can be loaded with unhealed trauma. While perceptions are necessary to help us understand and navigate our world, we can make a conscious choice not to be a victim or paralyzed by it. By being objective, aware, and mindful we can examine, release, and create our perceptions to support our peace and happiness.

In this current age of reality TV, addictive electronic devices, email, and social media, we have chosen to receive specific information from the world that feeds our perception in consistently confusing sound bites and visual memes. We are frequently visualizing what large corporations with an aim of persistently branding their products control us to see and believe. We are exercising less and less the analytical part of our perception that supports our wellbeing. The amazing retina is transferring visual information to our brain that is preprogrammed to serve the agenda of sources in power, including for-profit companies. In the same way we diet and focus our awareness on food intake, we can choose to consciously be aware of what we feed our perception and diet where appropriate. More importantly, we can take advantage of those amazing retinas in our eyes, intentionally concentrating more time focusing on all of what is there to perceive. Take a brave step with me toward being aware and consciously creating a wise and healthy *perceptive filter*.

Coaching and Perception—Perceptive Filter on Steroids

How do we approach the perceptive conundrum? Don Miguel Ruiz shares in his book *The Voice of Knowledge*, "It is our nature to make up stories, to interpret everything we perceive. Without awareness, we give our personal power to the story, and the story writes itself. With awareness, we recover the control of our story. We see we are the authors and if we don't like it we can change it." If we were the receivers and creators of our *perceptive filter*, then we already have the power to change it. Lau Tzu shared his wisdom in the *Tao Te Ching*, written over 2500 years ago, "At the center of your being you have the answer. You know who you are and you know what you want." We are aligning with our inner self when we consciously listen to our own wisdom and integrate that into our perceptions. Many current personal development leaders write about *empowerment* like it's a vitamin supplement. I chose to see power with a different *perceptive filter*. I believe we all have innate power, we are choosing not to connect with it much of the time. We observe people's power when, without thinking, they pull a person from a burning vehicle. We observe power in strangers who rescue people from flood waters, knowingly risking their lives. We observe power in first responders who assert their training over their fear to save lives. That *POWER* and drive to serve is in all of us and can, with intention, discipline, and support, be consciously accessed at times other than emergencies. Are you aware of the personal perceptive conundrum that is holding you back from accessing your power?

Neuroscientists have confirmed that patterns in the brain can be changed with consistent affirmative practices. When you acknowledge the need for a *perceptual filter* change in your life, but feel stuck, confused, or overwhelmed, coaching is the perfect solution. For individuals that have underlying emotional or mental health issues, coaching can be applied in tandem with professional mental health treatment or grief counseling. Partnering with a coach to do a deep dive into your core strengths and create a custom, manageable plan, unleashes your innate power ensuring lasting change. Kick that perceptual conundrum to the curb! Commit to consciously making a shift in your perceptions so they serve you. Take the step to treat yourself to a personal coaching assessment now, you will be amazed how powerful you already are.

Walk gently onto the *ice* of life and ponder these questions:

1. What are the messages in my head that limit me?
2. Who made those rules?
3. Do I have the courage to entertain that my current perceptions may not be true?
4. Do I hold tightly to perceptions that don't serve me and am I open to change?
5. What are my real strengths and weaknesses and how do I align with them?

Meet Kathleen A. Carr

Kathleen A. Carr, Certified Professional Life Transition Coach

I am a Certified Professional Coach, a writer, an entrepreneur, a survivor, and a wise sage. I have had thirty years of multiple successful careers as a Nurse, Contract Negotiator, Employee Advocate, Certified Mediator, and currently a Life and Career Coach engaging with professionals in life transitions.

I have expertise in Core Value testing, a tool which I integrate in my coaching programs. This tool measures the client's innate core values or primary energy drivers and is based in Abraham Maslow's theory of the *true inner self.* My passion is to work with professional clients facing transition to access their innate power and shift their perceptions to experience the possibilities for their lives.

I am a firm believer that we do not *empower* people, we redirect them to the power that already exists within them. Give yourself the gift of working with me to open a window into who you really are, shift perceptions that no longer serve you, and achieve peace.

Real change is belief in possibilities; not a rush to achievement, but faithfully and intentionally creating momentum.

Connect with me:

- kathleenacarr.com
- facebook.com/claimingpeace
- Twitter: @claimingpeace
- kathleen@claimingpeace.com

EIGHTEEN

Life's Purpose

YOUR TRUTH, SERVING, AND PARTICIPATION

By Tracy Brown

GREETINGS PHENOMENAL, one of a kind, gifted-person of the world, let me introduce myself to you. My name is Tracy Tinnette Brown and I'm a Certified Professional Life Coach. One of my many passions, as well as my mission in life, is to help you to win at discovering your purpose and passion and delivering it to others.

The reason why I decided to get certified as a life coach was to be true to myself, which allows me to motivate and inspire people. I feel that we are all unique, creative entities, and every so often we need to revamp in order to arrive at our designated calling. My revamp went into effect on my birthday this year. I was disappointed with myself because in my twenties I started working in a career I loved and I knew I was in the right place, doing the right thing. Somewhere in my thirties, I became consciously aware that there was something else that I was supposed to be doing. I kept myself locked into my original career even though I knew mentally and felt emotionally, that it was over.

For twenty-seven years my career had been business-to-business phone sales and marketing of products and services in many different industries. I also managed, supervised, recruited, trained, interviewed, and hired candidates. These are wonderful skills to have to be successful in just about any career and are skills that will forever serve me. I'm grateful and very proud of myself because for a long time this is how I stood proudly.

When my tenure ended, I did not know how to leave my career even though my passion was no longer there. I discovered I couldn't be satisfied continuing to be a sales and marketing business consultant when I knew I was no longer that. I recognized a new truth within me. I was overlooking my phenomenal, fabulous, divinely-bestowed gifts. I recognized that in order for me to serve, as requested by the universe, I had to make a change. In my new career as a life coach, I am now utilizing my strong communication and marketing skills to develop my business.

Sometimes we just need to get out of our own way to understand where we are supposed to be and what we are supposed to be undertaking. It can be fearsome to let go of what you have known for so long and what you have been great at. What's even more frightening is *not* venturing into what you know is 100% you and instead, holding on to what doesn't bring you happiness or resonate with you anymore.

You've been given many gifts and abilities unlike anyone else. There isn't another you in the world and this alone should inspire you to act on your bestowed greatness for the betterment of yourself and others. I believe that your participation in life, utilizing your gifts, talents, and special abilities are your legacy. If you serve others in need, with your own unique gifts, you will be highly rewarded by the universe, your higher-power/God.

Life is a clarifying progression, full of unexpected twists and turns. I have traveled many bumpy roads and I've made lots of u-turns in order to understand my purpose and position in life. If you are a student who is paying attention to everyday life lessons, you are always advancing in the class of life.

When you are willing to get out of your own way and let go of what was, or what you think should have been, you will discover positioning yourself to live the life of your dreams is not mind-boggling. Stop making yourself unhappy and just do you. The more conscious we are and the more in alignment we are with our truth, the greater world we can create. The universe is in the business of rewarding those that show up and do as they are divinely-appointed. The universe gave you a specific gift for you to shine among others to strengthen them. When you are of service to others, you cannot even imagine the multitude of gifts that the universe will bestow upon you.

Don't follow another's path, if that path is not truly yours, as it will likely result in pain and suffering. Your heart knows your truth. Listening to the wants and needs of your heart will always steer you in the right direction. There isn't another you in the world and this alone should inspire you to act on your greatness for the betterment of yourself and others.

I am proud to say that, I have the power within to continue to seek my truth and happiness which starts with me. I am very insightful and forever a student to life lessons. With what I have experienced and learned, I have matured into a teacher for others. I will be your personal cheerleader in all situations that you are dreaming up. I want you to win big in all ways for always.

What is your calling? What legacy will you leave behind for others to incorporate? How can you help others have less of a struggle? Will you participate fully as you should with what you were given by the powers that be, the universe/God? You are so needed in this world to rise up and exhibit your gifts and abilities. We are waiting on you to delight us. Won't you please come and be of service to all of us?

Meet Tracy Brown

Tracy Tinnette Brown is a certified professional life coach through Wainwright Global, a writer for Quora Digest and a radio talk show host/producer. Tracy has been motivating and inspiring people to prosper in the manner in which they are meant to, starting in her thirties. She has a knack for finding engaging resources to assist you when you are ready to elevate from phase A to B of your life to ensure that you arise to the new you. She is fully invested and passionate about wanting to help people transform so that they can manifest their purpose-filled life and may be content, utilizing their gifts and abilities to serve others. Tracy currently resides in Cumming, Georgia (a suburb of Atlanta) with her husband and mother.

You may contact Tracy seven days a week for inspirational and motivating speaking to individuals or groups, by phone, 678-663-4869 or Skype tracy-brown333. Her email address is ttb500@yahoo.com.

Be sure to call Tracy to receive your free gift of a one-on-one fifteen minute motivational session. Speak to Tracy about her becoming your personal life coach.

NINETEEN

Coaching Yourself to an Amazing Life

By Dr. Allen Barham

DO you believe you deserve to live an amazing life? Is happiness for you? Have you beaten yourself up over making the same costly mistakes? Do you wish to find the "Holy Grail" of how to live your personal life of fulfillment, happiness, success, peace, and healthy relationships? If you answered, "Yes!" or even, "I think so," you owe it to yourself to read the information I am going to share with you here; it will propel you forward on your journey to an amazing life.

First, let me exclaim the virtues of hiring a Life Coach to help you navigate the rocky, foggy, wet, dark terrain of finding and living an amazing life. However, jumpstart your quest using yourself as your personal Life Coach. Then, search for the right person to help you take your journey to the next level. You should get a qualified individual to help you process your thoughts, motives, and actions, and show you how to bring your life into harmony with your dreams. However, you are the expert on you; therefore, it is a wise decision to begin your life journey exploration yourself. I do not make any assertions that the tools and skills I am about to share with you are easy to implement; however, I will assert my confidence that these tools and skills will enable you to position yourself for purpose and happiness beyond your expectations. How can I make such a claim? Because, for the past twenty plus years, I have utilized the techniques and skills I am about to teach you. They continue to work in my life; I am one of the happiest, fulfilled, purposeful people I know. Let's get started!

Dispel Negative Self-Thoughts

One of the first steps you must take to move forward with your life of purpose and fulfillment is cast down negative self-beliefs. Feelings of inadequacy and self-doubt are toxic agents to every positive, healthy, and good thing you desire. Your self-beliefs influence the decisions you make in your life. If you believe you are underserving of wealth you will sabotage yourself away from wealth opportunities. If you believe you always pick the wrong mate, you will sabotage every good relationship. The examples could go on ad nauseam, but you get the point. Your mindset is critical to how you live and experience your life. The "glass half full, half empty" metaphor is applicable here. Ask yourself how you see situations and circumstances; do you imagine the "best case scenario" or the worst possible outcome? That is a powerful self-awareness exercise. Did you do it? No, why not? Take a moment and do that exercise. Finished? Great, you have just completed your first self-coaching session. Congratulations.

Make Your Life Amazing

Let me start off with the bad news. You will never experience an amazing life until you change the things, in your life, that destroy amazing. Self-evaluation and self-awareness are critical components for creating the amazing life you desire and deserve. Ask yourself, "What negative self-beliefs do I internalize?" You must be willing to be honest with yourself. You are your own personal coach and you have agreed to confidentiality, so be open. Coaches ask profound and probing questions. Think of some questions you would want a coach to ask you. What would you hope your coach sees about you that you are afraid to deliberately show? Ask yourself that question and many more questions that prompt answers you find difficult to disclose to other people. Allowing yourself to feel uncomfortable with exploring such questions is a major step towards identifying some of your personal roadblocks to living an amazingly happy and fulfilled life. Make a conscious decision to coach yourself through the initial steps of creating your amazing life. Then, reach out to a professional coach to help take you to the next level.

Know Yourself

"And this above all, to thine own self be true, and it must follow, as the night the day, thou canst not then be false to any man" (Shakespeare); this is my favorite saying of all time. All too often we have attached ourselves to the opinions and beliefs of others. Faulty formative teachings by well-meaning parental figures have caused many of us to internalize other people's belief systems and behavior patterns. Much of the internal conflicts we struggle with are due to anxiety over breaking free from beliefs and ideas not our own.

Who are you? Sticking with the paradigm of a coach, ask yourself this consistently profound and perplexing "open-ended" question; "Who am I?" What images come to mind? Your parents' child? Your children's parent? Friend, co-worker, supervisor, employee, neighbor, or a myriad of additional external self-identifiers. Those are what I call, "Possessive Identifiers"; each one has you tied to something external, and wedded to the external attachment there is no self-identity.

In my book, *LIVE Your LifePurpose*, I coined a phrase, "Triangular questioning process." This is a self-coaching technique where you ask yourself three, what I consider to be critical questions: "Who am I?"—"What is my purpose in this life?"—"Do I believe my purpose is given to me by my Creator?" While these questions do embrace the spiritual yearning and hunger of all humans, they are not designed to be religious or mystical.

Who Am I?

We all seek to find a profound meaning and purpose for our lives. However, most people seek purpose and meaning without first learning who they are. How can you know what you truly want to do if you do not know who you truly are?

Who are you? Take a moment and separate yourself from the ideas of your parents, friends, job, spouse, kids, money, neighbors, and pets. Be in a virtual space with nothing and no one there to add anything at all. The space is blank. What would you create? What are you seeing in the dark empty space where you exist? What do you want around you? Do you see trees or buildings—or both? Do you see yourself on the water or on land? What are you doing to pass the time away? Come on, think hard! Be creative! Think back to when you were little and you found your private space to fanta-size about what you imagined being a grownup was like. Now, think about your rebellious stage. What were the things you hated but were forced to participate in nonetheless? Search out the things that make you feel uniquely "you." That is the beginning of your self-exploration coaching.

What Is My Purpose in This Life?

Fill in your empty, blank, dark space with all the things you believe would add meaning and purpose to your life. Think about what inspires you to become more than an employee, a parent, a sibling, someone's child, friend, or boss. What keeps you up at night wondering, "What if I had just...?" The late Dr. Myles Munroe said cemeteries are some of the most valuable real estate in the world because of all the potential buried there. Many people live most of their lives brooding over what might have been. Others cower in fear over the possibility of being inadequate or unaccepted. Still others merely talk about what they intend to do—"When..." You must make a conscious decision to embrace a life of purpose; even if you do not know exactly what that purpose is now, you must decide to live a life you choose to live, based on finding or fulfilling your idea of purpose. Here is what we call "the miracle question": when you finish reading this chapter or book, if you are living the life of your dreams, what would have changed for you?

Do I Believe My Life Purpose Is Given to Me by My Creator?

The answer here depends on your belief in a Creator or who the role you believe a "higher power" plays in your life. I do not have the space to offer a theological treatise here.

TAKE the Steps

Identify the roadblocks that keep popping up! Can you identify the times in your life when you felt like you were ready to take on the world? What did that feel like? What was happening to induce such a feeling of invincibility? A new idea or new job that sparked a sense of hope and change can often create a feeling of excitement. Did something happen that caused that feeling of euphoria to dissipate or die? If so, what happened? What stopped you from continuing down the road to absolute fulfillment and success? The dreaded roadblocks. Every amazing building structure, bridge, or highway, was once just a big roadblock to someone's idea or dream. Someone will look at a forest and determine, there are too many trees and rocks for anyone to live or shop here. However, someone else will have a dream of people living and shopping in that exact location and say, "All I need to do is chop down those trees and bulldoze those boulders, and I can create a great living experience." When confronted with the road less traveled or no road at all, get fired up to knock down the trees that block your view of happiness. Be determined to bulldoze life's debris from your path. If there is no road, make one!

Eliminate the noise from your life! Perhaps you struggle with voices in your head telling you how things "are supposed to be" or reminding you "it has always been done this way." One of the major factors keeping people back from pursuing their dreams and aspirations is the noise of other people in their head. Well-meaning but misguided family members and friends can cause you to turn over your passion to their belief system or opinion. If you ever hope to experience the amazing life you think about, you must begin to eliminate the noise. Come on coach, ask yourself whose voice rings the loudest in your head that stops you from taking chances to follow your dreams. What people keep screaming to you that you are crazy to believe you can change the world? It is imperative that you eliminate the noise that is funneling into your psyche. Naysayers will say "Nay" to every great and powerful pursuit you attempt. Eliminate the noise! Clear your head of negative voices.

Prepare yourself for an amazing life! Do not allow yourself to get trapped in the guilt syndrome of other people complaining about how selfish you are. Most people who complain do not produce anything monumental. Start with small steps, but start. Give people back their problems, issues, responsibilities, and beliefs. Ask yourself, "What am I willing to do to live an amazing life?" Then contact me, Dr. B at, drbmeok@aol.com.

Meet Dr. Allen C. Barham, Sr. (Dr. B)

Dr. B is the founder, Sr. Pastor, and Chief Presiding Prelate of Destiny Driven Ministries International, Inc. (DDM). Dr. B is the owner of DayMaster Enterprises, LLC (gomastertheday.com).

Dr. B is a high school dropout, but a self-described education "drop-in." He obtained his GED, and then continued to higher education. He is a graduate of Ashworth University, AS, Psychology; Bellevue University, BS, Behavioral Science; The Jacksonville Theological Seminary, PhDs in Christian Psychology, Clinical Christian Counseling, Christian Education, and a Doctorate in Theology.

Dr. B is a licensed Clinical Christian Counselor certified in the following disciplines: Violence, Substance Abuse, Marriage and Family Maintenance, Individual/Group Crisis Management, and Adolescent and Youth (Individual & Group) Counseling. He is also a licensed Pastoral Counselor, and Certified Life, Purpose, Relationship, and Success Coach.

Dr. B is an author of two books: *Remember, It Is Your Charge, Go Master The Day,* and *LIVE Your LifePurpose,* available in book stores and on Amazon.com in both print and Kindle form.

Dr. B is happily married to Vicki, and considers her, Ministry, and their children as his greatest loves.

TWENTY

The Exquisite Journey from the Head to the Heart

By Linda Gallicchio

IN 1991, I had been married for 17 years. I had two beautiful children, Michael and Katie, a job, a lovely home, and a deep connection to family and friends. If asked I would tell you, I was living the "American Dream." Then one day, yes in one day, my world would come crashing down on me and my family. I began experiencing memories of childhood sexual abuse.

Even as a child, I knew there were a myriad of secrets that were buried inside of me that I did not want to acknowledge. I had pushed the memories and the associated feelings deep within to survive. I felt like I hated myself all the time. I always wondered if the following was happening to my friends too:

- Were they also so filled with self-loathing that they had zero confidence in their ability to navigate their world?

- Were they always checking the emotional temperature in the house to see if it was free from anger?
- Did they have to "protect" their siblings and mother from experiencing their father's wrath?
- Did they wet their underwear on occasion until they were twelve years old, and then hide them because they were ashamed and embarrassed?
- Did they insist people not sneak up from behind and say boo?
- Did they have anxiety and a sense of doom that accompanied them every single day?
- And last but not least: Did they lay awake in the darkness making believe they were sleeping, all the while knowing that he was lurking in the hallway?

Those memories poured out of my subconscious mind like lava, molten rock and magma, flowing from a volcano, thick and rich with sediment, slowly, steadily, destroying everything in its path and seemingly never-ending. There was a switch in my brain that would signal a memory was coming. When the switch was activated, I felt fear and the agony of knowing that I was going to re-experience the hell that my body went through one more time. Both as a child and as an adult, my spirit/soul would find a way out of my physical body. This is called disassociation. Dissociative symptoms can potentially disrupt every area of mental functioning. Examples of dissociative symptoms include the experience of detachment or feeling as if one is outside one's body. Dissociative disorders are frequently associated with previous experience of trauma.[1]

The memories came so fast they caused my mind to break from reality. It took years to get my footing because of all the grief, the anger, sadness, rivers of tears, and forgiveness, and I finally reached a state of acceptance and became whole. This said, the healing and growing does go on forever.

If you have ever experienced anything similar, I want you to know that you can make the journey from the head to the heart that will unblock old beliefs and feelings. You will find the answers in your heart where the divine resides. It takes focus, practice, and patience. The messages from your heart can be your answer to living the life you have always dreamed of.

My transformation began, while I was attending codependence anonymous meetings (CODA). CODA is for those who need to work on their relationships with friends and family as all of us do from time to time. At speaker meetings we are asked to share about our experience, strength, and hope.

As I stood up to speak and looked around the room, I felt a shift in my head, like we were in a different dimension, where we had all shed our physical bodies. It happened in a second and I had the distinct feeling that we were all one and connected; not separate. It was a euphoric feeling. As soon as I became consciously aware of what was happening, the feeling vanished. It was such a profound experience that I knew I had to find out what happened.

I learned to call my experience "a moment of grace." I learned that we all have access to this grace, which allows us to know for certain that we are greater than we could possibly know. There is much to be discovered about our inner-world through our senses.

Thousands of years ago, our ancestors used their senses to survive. We now call those senses intuition. They used intuition in their lives to escape danger, "see" what was coming in the future, to "hear" whispers of guides and angels ushering them on their path and to "feel" or "know" if something was not right. These skills are still taught and practiced by the American Indians and some

Eastern Religions. I want you to know that you have the same intuitive capability to guide your life, to become more alive, joyful, happy, and loving. Yes, I'm talking to you.

The definition of intuition is: inner guidance, inner voice, intelligence from the heart (not the head). Intuition comes from the energy of the heart. Our hearts "speak" to us in various ways to live our lives more fully. Our hearts are our inner-teacher as opposed to our external-teacher. Intuition is a direct-knowing that comes through your heart. Your divine self is innate and tells you what is true for you. To access your intuition you need to be open, receptive, and curious enough to explore. And yes, it takes time and patience to cultivate these skills.

When you ask a question of the universe, or God, then you need to discern through your senses or intuitive skills what the answer is. Your answers do not come as talking to you like they do in the physical world. Your answers come to you maybe in a song. Maybe in what someone says to you. Maybe in a book you are reading. If you know this and are aware that this will happen you will open yourself to the answers you seek.

Intuition is a metaphysical skill. If you are familiar with metaphysics (beyond physics) you will know that energy is infinite and EVERYWHERE; beside you, inside of you, and everything is made of energy. To tap into that energy, you can use your senses. There are four different sense modalities that you can use to tap into the infinite information stream. Access to this information will serve you for the rest of your life. Why? To give you information about what you should do next or what your life might look like in the future. Sometimes the information you receive will be a message for someone else (it could be tricky deciding whether or not to tell that person).

Here are the four modalities:

1. Clairvoyance—Clear sight. You are able to see pictures in your mind's eye. Some people call them "visions." You may "see" an old memory or "see" a future probability that may happen. You may even "see" a running movie of events. The visions may come as flashes, like still pictures, of things connected to the information coming through.

2. Clairaudient—Clear hearing. Inner listening, whispers in your ear, voices, and yes, you are not crazy. Some people can "hear" voices and it is all part of our mastery of skills in this human lifetime. You know the voice you "hear" is true when the message resonates as truth within your innate heart.

3. Clairsentience—Clear sensing or feeling. You can sense or feel the energy of your environment. You easily pick up on how other people are feeling. A lot of people with this modality can be overwhelmed with others' feelings and have to protect themselves. You have a keen knack for sensing what is going on with someone without them telling you.

4. Claircognizant—Clear knowing. You have an inner knowing. You make a statement and someone asks, "How do you know that?" You may answer, "I don't know. I just do." Your inner-self is telling you something you know to be true.

See if you can determine which "clair" speaks to you the most. Ask yourself:

- When you need or want information how does it come to you?
- Does it come as a visual picture?
- Do you hear the answer through an inner voice?
- Do you have a feeling about the answer?

- Or do you just know the answer even if you don't know how?

Think of a situation where you had to make a decision. Which "clair" determined your answer?

When we trust our intuition to give us the right answer and engage in meditation, journaling, exercise, and other mindful practices, we will become more in charge of our own path and create a more loving, compassionate, kind environment in which to live. Remember one person can affect the whole world by knowing yourself and living a more calm and peaceful life.

Reflecting back, it was a long journey, one full of lessons and love, laughter and tears, angst and grace. Today, my life is different. Today, I feel fulfilled. I feel loved. I feel good enough.

Meet Linda Gallicchio, CMC

Linda Gallicchio is a devoted wife of forty-three years, mother of two loving, successful adult children, an amazing daughter-in-law, and a grandmother to three precious grandchildren. She is an author, speaker, and master coach who has trained over 4,000 coaches during her tenure with Wainwright Global Institute of Professional Coaching (WGI).

Linda has studied metaphysics for decades and is always searching for the meaning behind life's mysteries. She co-wrote the Certified Spiritual Coach (CSC) course with Barbara Wainwright and with her vast knowledge of spirituality, she will engage you with her quick wit and candor.

Linda currently teaches the CSC course through WGI. In the CSC course, you will learn all about the four "clairs," all things relating to spirituality including meditation, pendulum reading, oracle cards, essential oils, quartz crystals, centering tools, reincarnation, and how to apply those skills and tools as a coach.

Because spirituality is pervasive in our lives you will also answer questions such as: How do I connect with Spirit/God/Universe? Am I willing to forgive myself? You will learn about your life's purpose, universal oneness, living in the moment, being in the flow, and law of attraction. She also invites you to email or call with any questions you have about life coaching or spiritual coaching. She is also available for coaching anyone who would like to expand their consciousness about themselves.

To enroll in her course, use this URL wainwrightglobal.com/linda.htm

You can contact Linda at 818-257-8480 or send her an email at lindagallicchio@live.com.

References:

1. https://www.psychiatry.org/patients-families/dissociative-disorders/what-are-dissociative-disorders

TWENTY-ONE

The Power of Coaching

By Barbara Wainwright

WHAT IS the process and purpose of coaching and how does coaching affect true transformation within yourself and others?

In the dynamic role of being a coach, we have the privilege of helping others to live a fulfilling and purpose-filled life. And of course, if everybody was living from that beautiful place within, I believe we would have peace on Earth. (*There's some insight into my ultimate goal.*)

Not long ago, the main perception of coaching was limited to the sports coaching field. Now the profession is growing across a variety of niches. Life coaching, business coaching, and executive coaching are now popular and mainstream. In fact, there are now over fifty coaching niches; all of them are powerful to help bring people into alignment with their purpose.

The object of coaching is to inspire people to

- do some inner-work to discover their purpose in life;
- gain clarity on what they most desire to create and accomplish in life;
- strategically design what they want to see occur in their life;
- develop plans and take action to manifest their transformation.

We facilitate clients to dig deep into their own beliefs and encourage them to ditch limiting beliefs and goals they've adopted from others. For example, instead of pursuing what their parents always dreamed for them, our clients are asked to contemplate what they believe would be the best expression of their individuality.

Once they have identified what they're born to do, we encourage, motivate, inspire, and hold them accountable to moving forward to the optimum experience they're here to create.

I would say that life coaching is about the bringing people into alignment with their life's purpose. What could be better than helping others realize and live their divine purpose?

We want our clients to uncover what their heart is calling them to do:

- What are they passionate about?
- What are they inspired to do?
- What change, cause, or effect do they want to create in the world?
- When they die, what legacy do they want to leave to future generations?

I believe we each inherently have a blueprint; an innate human design with a specific purpose or intention. We're all here to affect something, to cause something. If we are willing to dive deep enough, the reason we are here bubbles up from inside of us. Our passion, our purpose, may have been buried inside of us, just waiting to be exposed to the light of day. And when it comes to the surface the entire universe rejoices in the newly unleashed possibilities.

Manifesting Your Destiny

When you begin to take steps towards manifesting and/or creating what is inside of you that you're naturally called to express—that's when an inner-joy occurs, an inner-peace. That's when you'll recognize that you're walking the path which is aligned toward your highest good. Your intuition will begin to lead you toward a life where your heart, mind, and soul are fully expressing their magnificence.

With the Wainwright Global Method of Coaching, we help our clients experience a richly rewarding life by creating a vision statement. In our terms, a vision statement is a powerful, affirmative statement of our client's dreams and goals, written as if those goals have already occurred. With a vision statement our clients have a clear picture of exactly where they want to go, what they want to do, and what it looks like when they have arrived. The vision statement is an acknowledgement of our clients' dreams in living color.

As a life coach, during our first interview, we ask our clients to explore multiple facets of their life, such as financial, professional, relationships, emotional, spiritual, health, and wellness. We ask clarifying questions and combine the client's answers to create a positive, affirmative statement where our clients can easily and naturally envision themselves moving toward their goals with ease and grace. It is an honor to get to know our clients this profoundly and it creates a wonderful rapport. Often during the first coaching session with a client, we become aware that it is the first time our client has been fully witnessed, fully heard, and then acknowledged.

I believe the vision statement is vital to a person's success. If it was simple and easy to change, to step out of our comfort zones, we would all be living the life of our dreams. Change is difficult for most of us because we have a built-in mechanism for our survival, called homeostasis. Homeostasis is our innate drive to remain in a calm physiological state. It doesn't matter how smart you are, if your subconscious is not on board with your new plan, it isn't going to happen. Why? Because our fight or flight mechanisms kick in when we do something that is out of our normal routine and before long, we will have sabotaged our plans and end up right back where we started—in our comfort zone. Is the comfort zone comfortable? Not always; however, when venturing into the unknown, whatever that may be, the internal drive to stay with your norm may override your drive to succeed.

Now for the good news! While listening to your vision statement you are restructuring the neural synapses in your brain, creating new neural-pathways as you mentally see, hear, touch, taste, and feel how you will be celebrating success as your new life unfolds. The vision statement is the key to this transformational process, as it helps to reprogram your subconscious mind to be in sync with your optimal destination.

When we are walking our divine path, the Universe/ God/ Higher-Mind conspires on our behalf to bring everything we need into alignment for our new story to unfold. I believe when we're acting in accordance with the Universe/ God/ Higher-Mind we attract the right people and events so that everything comes easily and naturally to us. Therefore, if you are struggling, I recommend you take a closer look at your plan and your actions, because struggle means something is out of sync with your path. The vision statement will help you stay on your divinely inspired journey as it reinforces your intentions and causes you to stay centered, balanced, and in alignment with your mission.

Because the vision statement creates such a solid foundation, giving you the confidence you need to move forward, when your friends and family ask if you've lost your mind and gone crazy, it will be easy for you to dismiss the negativity and opposition from entering your mindset. You will have a new freedom to know, do, and be true to yourself.

The vision statement isn't simply a list of affirmations. In fact, I don't believe affirmations truly work. If an affirmation doesn't resonate with you, your critical conscious mind is going to reject it immediately. The ideas won't be accepted into your subconscious mind, which is the place that everything manifests from. There's an important distinction between a Wainwright Global vision statement and a typical affirmation. The vision statements that our coaches create for their clients are tailor-made for them. We're very careful to use the language of the client—not our language—specifically the language of the client. When they hear their vision statement, they're hearing their dreams described in the words they use daily, so the message sounds and feels natural and true for them. This causes a mind-shift (the reprogramming of the neural-pathways, creating new neural synapses) as they continue to listen, and this is when transformation begins.

Here's some more good news. Because your thoughts are now lining up with your dreams and goals, you will soon discover that changes occur quickly and in seemingly miraculous ways. Clients may start with six-month or one-year goals; however, with the vision statement as their secret sauce, and accountability by the coach, they're so on-point and focused that they're meeting their goals at a pace much faster than they ever imagined.

Coaching vs. Therapy

The therapy process delves into a person's history, while coaching is a present-time, forward-thinking process. In my opinion, therapy was important for the psychological evolution of our species. It was a way for us to look back and figure out how different family systems or environments impacted us and helped us to address what we could do better for greater end-results. I believe that we are now at a turning-point, where it's time to put aside the past difficulties, focus on the present and strive to attain our future goals. It's time to uncover our passions and accomplish our dreams. Coaching helps you take stock of your present strengths, dive into your passions, and live a purpose-driven life.

Wainwright Global Method of Coaching

If you think coaching may be an avenue you wish to pursue, you will be delighted to know that becoming a coach is not difficult. With Wainwright Global's highly-interactive, two-day intensive coach training course, and our coaching system and methodology, you will learn exactly how to coach clients to success. In fact, you will have coached a client through their first, second, and third coaching sessions before leaving the class. And, you will have also experienced coaching from the client side of the table so you will be aware of just how powerful this coaching system really is. And lastly, because you will be learning a system of coaching, you can begin coaching in any niche you choose, for example: relationship coaching, weight loss coaching, recovery coaching, or spiritual coaching.

In Closing

My greatest desire is to see everyone living a purpose-filled life, engaged in their passion, while making a positive difference in the world. Surround yourself with people who are like-minded and have the same aspirations. That way, you'll have the opportunity to experience a collective manifestation rather than an individual manifestation and things will happen faster and grander for you and your colleagues.

In the words of Marianne Williamson, "Who are you not to be brilliant, gorgeous, talented, and fabulous? We are all meant to shine as children do. You were born to make manifest the glory of God that is within you." Until next time, be spontaneous: do the things you are called to do, take charge of your life. And remember, when you show up for God, God will show up for you, in miraculous ways.

Meet Barbara Wainwright

Barbara Wainwright, the CEO and Founder of Wainwright Global, Inc., has dedicated her life to being of service to others. Barbara's life experiences have led her on a path of self-discovery and higher learning in her personal quest to make the world a better place for her family, her friends, and her clients.

As a single mother when she was younger, Barbara began her quest to help others succeed by sharing her knowledge and experience she gained from running a software company for twenty years. She believes that every person has a life purpose. And that once a person discovers their purpose and begins taking steps towards actualizing that purpose, a new level of confidence slowly unveils itself, many different forms of abundance become realized, and inner-peace begins its evolutionary process.

Barbara is best known for training over 6,000 professional coaches since 2006 and has established credibility in the marketplace through acquiring accreditation at the graduate university level through Strategic Learning Alliance, an applied-learning credentialing organization who confers the CPC® credential of Wainwright Global's Certified Professional Coaches.

You can reach Barbara at 800-711-4346 or Barbara@Wainwright-Global.com. You can learn more about Wainwright Global's coaching courses at LifeCoachTrainingOnline.com. Download a free book about 52 Coaching Niches here: lifecoachtrainingonline.com/content/freebook.

Afterword

We trust you have enjoyed reading these coaching stories and that you have been inspired in some way to move forward in your own life. Hiring a coach may be one of the best moves you can make to ultimately have the breakthroughs to your personal success that you deserve.

If you are contemplating becoming a coach, we recommend you contact Wainwright Global Institute of Professional Coaching for your education and certification.

Wainwright Global Institute of Professional Coaching currently offers courses in Professional, Spiritual, Recovery, Relationship, Group, NLP, and Career Coaching.

Wainwright Global Institute of Professional Coaching
LifeCoachTrainingOnline.com
800-711-4346